FOR WHO T

David Marsh is the production editor of the *Guardian*, which he joined in 1996. He edits the newspaper's style guide and *Mind Your Language* blog. He learned about grammar and spelling at Poynton County Primary School, Cheshire, and later attended King's School, Macclesfield, Sheffield University, and University College London. He started his career at the Kent Messenger Group and edited the *Redditch Indicator* and *Bromley & Bexley Leader* (both, sadly, defunct) before joining the *Independent* (which is still going). He also worked for the *Financial Times* – the result, he believes, of mistaken identity. He lives in Berkshire.

Further praise for *For Who the Bell Tolls*:

'David Marsh … is better placed than most to offer a practical guide to writing, and he is not shy of taking witty sideswipes at the competition … With admirable clarity, Marsh goes on to explain the gerund and subjunctive, the difference between comparing to and comparing with, and the correct use of the word "whom"… An entertaining compendium of usage notes and mini-essays.' Steven Poole, *Guardian*

'This isn't the snobby or stilted approach you might find associated with some other newspaper styles. Marsh's advice helps craft writing that sounds natural and is clear and concise.' Erin Brenner, *Copyediting*

'Serious yet light-hearted, personal but universal… A funnier book than is usual for the field … *For Who the Bell Tolls* blends respect for sound traditions with an embrace of new linguistic possibilities, and would make a welcome addition to any amateur or professional word-wrangler's shelf.' Stan Carey, *Sentence First*

'Marsh targets a point halfway between the cerebral cortex and the funny bone – and his aim is almost invariably true.' Ken Haley, *Australian*

For Who the Bell Tolls

Bell Tolls

The essential and entertaining
guide to grammar

DAVID MARSH

First published in Great Britain in 2013
by Guardian Books, Kings Place, 90 York Way, London N1 9GU
and Faber & Faber Ltd, Bloomsbury House,
74–77 Great Russell Street, London WC1B 3DA

This paperback edition first published in 2014

Typeset by seagulls.net
Printed and bound in the UK by CPI Group (UK) Ltd, Croydon, CR0 4YY

A CIP record for this book is available from the British Library

ISBN 978–1–783–35052–0

10 9 8 7 6 5 4

To Freddie, Al, Dom and Ol,
and in loving memory of Patrick

CONTENTS

Ballad of a Refuse Disposal Officer

Oh, my old man's a dustman, he wears a dustman's hat,
He wears cor blimey trousers and he lives in a council flat.
He looks a proper nana in his great big hobnail boots,
He's got such a job to pull them up that he calls them
daisy roots.

LONNIE DONEGAN

You have to ask probing questions of nature.
That's what is called experimentation, and then
you may get some answers that mean something.
Otherwise you just get junk.

NOAM CHOMSKY

It all started with Lonnie Donegan and the girl of my eight-year-old dreams. 'My Old Man's a Dustman' was not the first record I bought: that was Cliff Richard's 'The Young Ones'. It was, however, the first record I loved. Lonnie's irreverent tale of his father's adventures as a council binman was cheekily related in an exotic (to me, 200 miles north of London)

The tweets running along the bottom of the following pages are a small selection of the 11,000 or so shared by @guardianstyle and its followers since 2010.

cockney accent and full of fascinatingly arcane language – 50 years later, I still don't know what 'cor blimey trousers' are, and I don't want to know: it might break the spell.

I became so obsessed with the song that I even began to wish my own old man were a dustman, rather than a telephone engineer. And not only because it would mean I could stop trying to justify my claims that while serving in the Royal Air Force (true), he had been a Spitfire pilot during the Battle of Britain (untrue). How hilarious it would have been when Dad came home to take off his dustman's hat and hobnail boots and regale us with tales of his life as what the song's subtitle ironically called a 'refuse disposal officer'.

I knew I just had to perform this song live at the class Christmas concert organised by our teacher, the glamorous Mrs Birtles. My big problem, apart from a lack of instruments and talent – which I reckoned I could bluff my way through – was finding a sidekick to enable me to crack Lonnie's jokes. Sample:

'My dustbin's absolutely full of toadstools.'
'How do you know it's full?'
'Because there's not mushroom inside!'

I asked all the boys in the class but, rightly fearing that they might make fools of themselves, they turned me down. I was too scared to ask the girls, and especially the girl I secretly loved: Clare, an ice-cool blonde with pale blue eyes who was the epitome of junior school style and sophistication. Admittedly, I didn't have much to go on – my mum, Mrs Birtles and Valerie Singleton of *Blue Peter* were my

@malchadwick 'Walk the talk': acceptable? Surely you are meant to talk the talk, then walk the walk?

only points of comparison – but to me, Clare was the perfect woman.

Imagine my astonishment, then, when in response to Mrs Birtles' appeal to the girls, who should volunteer to be the foil for my comic musical turn but … Clare herself. The gig was a fiasco – she was, naturally, word perfect and charmed our sceptical audience while I fluffed or forgot most of the lyrics – but it was what Clare said to me backstage afterwards that was to have a lasting impression. Trying to act casually, I spluttered out a feeble question: why had she agreed to be my straight man?

'Because you always come top in the spelling test.'

My spelling – the one thing I was any good at – had got me the girl!

Things didn't work out between Clare and me: it turned out that gauche eight-year-old geeks were not really her type (although this didn't prevent her equally lovely younger sister inexplicably agreeing to go out with a spottier, but still gauche and geeky, teenage me a few years later). But she taught me a valuable lesson. You have to make the most of what you are given in this life, and while my preferred career choices – footballer or rock star – would probably have been a more reliable route to getting girls, a flair for spelling (and, later, grammar) were what I had been given. They have been the basis of nearly four decades in journalism and a lifelong quest for grammatical perfection. Or, as you might regard it, messing about with other people's words to make them read better. This book is the result of that quest.

The late Nicholas Tomalin, a distinguished foreign correspondent, said the only qualities essential for success as a

@guardianstyle How about talking the talk, walking the walk, then tweeting the tweet?

journalist were 'rat-like cunning, a plausible manner, and a little literary ability'. He was right about the first two, but I'm not sure about the last one – I have worked with plenty of successful journalists I would not trust to write a shopping list. The phone-hacking scandal came as no surprise to most of us because anyone who has worked as a reporter knows that you would sell your grandmother into slavery if it helped you get a good story. When it comes to writing, however, journalists are like any other group of people: some are better than others. The less good ones rely on colleagues to translate their efforts into something you can publish with reasonable confidence that the person whose name appears on the story will not be pelted with rotten fruit by contemptuous readers.

I've spent my adult life working for newspapers, from Kent to Hong Kong, from the *Sun* to the *Financial Times*, from local weeklies that sold a few thousand copies to the *Guardian*, with its global readership of many millions. Among other jobs that no one else would do, I've been a ballet critic, football reporter, lonely hearts correspondent, restaurant reviewer and pop pundit. But editing has given me the greatest satisfaction: the satisfaction that only comes from turning the sow's ear of rough-and-ready reportage, written against a deadline, into a passable imitation of a silk purse, then putting a witty, apt or – at the very least – not inaccurate headline on it.

It's been a lifelong mission to create order out of chaos. And that's what I mean by a quest for perfection. The chaos takes many forms. It might be sloppy syntax, a disregard for grammar or a fundamental misunderstanding of what grammar is. It could be an adherence to 'rules' that have no real basis and get in the way of fluent, unambiguous communication at the expense of ones that are actually useful. Then there's chaos and confusion about punctuation – for which the poor greengrocer seems, rather unfairly, to get most of the blame – and spelling. The chaos is not random, however. Clear, honest use of English has many enemies: politicians, business and marketing people, local authority and civil service jargonauts, rail companies, estate agents, academics ... even some journalists. Thinking and writing in cliches, abusing and misusing language, assaulting us with gobbledegook, they are a powerful foe but we can beat them. I hope this book will help.

Let's face it: most grammar books are boring. This includes academic works couched in language so technical and arcane that they might have been written specifically to make the subject difficult to understand, much as people imagine (wrongly, as it happens) that the Qwerty keyboard was invented to slow down typists. In Shakespeare's *Henry VI Part 2*, Jack Cade says: 'Thou hast most traitorously corrupted the youth of the realm in erecting a grammar school.' If the old-fashioned grammar school I attended was in any way typical, it's true that only a few nerds such as me really enjoyed the English language lessons. It takes a particular kind of kid to look forward to clause analysis and precis as enthusiastically as I did.

No one taught us fun stuff, such as the fact that an apostrophe is the difference between a company that knows its shit and a company that knows it's shit, or the importance of capital letters to avoid ambiguity in such sentences as 'I helped my Uncle Jack off his horse'. But this is the grammar that people really need to know. And although there's not necessarily any harm in learning a little about form and function, noun phrases and adjuncts, binding theory and pseudo-cleft thematic ordering, on the whole we are more likely to repel the barbarians at the gate if we keep things nice and simple.

Chomsky, incidentally, was wrong about junk. He was dismissing the study of language that real people actually use, which he considers inferior to that used by theoretical linguists (sitting in an armchair, asking 'probing questions' about the language that real people actually use). Which brings me back to Lonnie Donegan, who was right about junk. I still listen to that record and when I do I am struck by how many of its pleasures are related to language: the cockney accent and rhyming slang ('daisy roots' – boots), the word-play-based humour, the gentle dig at local authority jargon ('Ballad of a Refuse Disposal Officer'). At eight, I knew that pop was fun. The King of Skiffle showed me that language could be fun, too.

Finally, a brief word about Muphry's law, the editorial application of Murphy's law ('If there are two or more ways to do something, and one of those ways can result in a catastrophe, then someone will do it'). Muphry's law states: 'If you write anything criticising editing or proofreading, there will be a fault of some kind in what you have written.' Quest for perfection or not, experience suggests this book is unlikely to be an exception to that maxim … so to save time: sorry for all the mistakes. Unlike the day I put the wrong price on the front page of the *Independent*, costing the company tens of thousands of pounds, I cannot blame them on a 'computer glitch'.

CHAPTER I

The Wages of Syntax

Grammar is glamorous, sexy and fun.
Don't think so? Read on

> *It will be proved to thy face that thou hast men*
> *about thee that usually talk of a noun and a verb,*
> *and such abominable words as no Christian ear can*
> *endure to hear.*
> WILLIAM SHAKESPEARE, *HENRY VI PART 2*

> *When you are applying the rules of grammar skilfully,*
> *you ascend to another level of the beauty of language.*
> MURIEL BARBERY

Whose photograph do you think is estimated to have appeared on the front page of the *Daily Telegraph* more than anyone else's? Margaret Thatcher? Tony Blair? The Queen Mother? Diana, Princess of Wales? Wrong. It's an accountant called Derek Derbyshire, who briefly signed to a modelling agency when he was out of work in the early 1960s. You've probably seen him: he appeared for years in the bottom right-hand corner of national newspaper front pages under headlines such as 'Why Are You Shamed By Your English?' and 'Why Does Your English Let You Down?' (He may also have doubled up as the worried-looking character who couldn't remember names and faces.) The advertisements, for a correspondence course called the Practical English Programme, were the longest running in newspaper history.

If you spent English lessons at school staring out of the window, scratching your name into the desk, or gazing wistfully at the object of your affections, you are in good company: hundreds of thousands of people decided they needed to take the course. But then people have always fretted about whether their grammar and vocabulary come up to snuff. Sorry, reach the required standard. 'The greater part of the world's troubles are due to questions of grammar,' according to the 16th-century essayist Michel de Montaigne. And he didn't have to contend with people pointing out his grammatical errors to the world in the comments below blogposts or on Twitter. The very word 'grammar' sounds dull. If only it were called something sexy, such as 'glamour'. Which is interesting, because the words are related: the Oxford English Dictionary (OED) says *glamour* was 'originally Scots … a corrupt form of *grammar*'.

But while language about language may sound off-putting, most professional writers and editors seem to get by without bothering too much about terminology. You don't need to know that 'this is he' is an example of the predicate nominative to be all too aware that someone who uses it to answer the phone is going to sound like a twerp. Linguistics can get very complex – some books written by the provisional wing of Noam Chomsky's barmy army look more like advanced mathematics than English. All I know is that X-bar theory has nothing to do with lap-dancing clubs. It doesn't need to be complicated. If someone tells you they have discovered an example of a kernel clause that is semantically or pragmatically exclamative, but syntactically declarative, just say: 'You did WHAT?'

@DuncanNRoss 'Cameron is an horrendous PM' your thoughts?

What Is Grammar?

I am free to confess that I don't know grammar.
Lady Blessington, do you know grammar?

BULWER LYTTON

When 900 years old you reach, look as good you will not,
hmmm?

YODA, *STAR WARS: EPISODE VI – RETURN OF THE JEDI*

So what is grammar? The American satirist Ambrose Bierce defined it drily as 'a system of pitfalls thoughtfully prepared for the feet of the self-made man'. A fair point. Grammar was taught to generations of children as a set of dos and don'ts, mainly the latter (don't start a sentence with a conjunction, don't end a sentence with a preposition, don't split an infinitive); and some books on the subject still read as if their aim is to make readers feel inferior because they are not sure what a gerund is. I can't think of any other subject that is approached in such a negative way. If you are teaching someone to play tennis, you don't spend all your time telling them not to hit the ball out or serve into the net, or all the other things they can't do; you show them how to serve, volley and smash – hard – and how if they do those things, they can really enjoy themselves.

It should be the same with grammar. Around the time of my unrequited love affair with Clare, I started a much more enduring relationship with language, thanks to a little book we were given called *The New First Aid in English*. To my astonishment, it is still in print, 50 years later, and I can

---

@guardianstyle Much as we agree with the sentiment
it should be 'a horrendous'.

still enjoy my favourite bits, such as 'Absurdities': 'Can you explain what is absurd in the following? *In some countries it is against the law for a man to marry his widow's sister.*' Some sections are flawless and the explanations clearer than in many grammar books for grownups.

One thing I didn't learn from *The New First Aid* is that the modern definition of grammar is the set of rules followed by speakers of a language. By rules I do not mean where to put an apostrophe, although we will come to such things in due course. I'm talking about the rules that every native English speaker – David Beckham, Kylie Minogue, Jay-Z, Her Majesty the Queen, you, me and 360 million or so other people around the world – instinctively understands. If, for example, the definition of grammar above read 'a set of language followed of rules by the speakers', a native speaker would recognise that, even if the words are the same, the order they are in breaks various rules of English. They did not learn this from a book, any more than they had to be taught that when you pronounce an address, the stress normally goes on the first word if it's a street (*Oxford* Street, *Victoria* Street, *Jump* Street), and on the last word if it's not (Abbey *Road*, Park *Lane*, Electric *Avenue*).

'The Coffee Song', a 1946 Frank Sinatra hit, contains the refrain 'They've got an awful lot of coffee in Brazil'. You only have to rearrange the words slightly to get 'they've got a lot of awful coffee in Brazil'; the point is not whether this is as hilarious as I thought when I discovered it at the age of six, but that from about 18 months children start to grasp that in English, word order is all-important (which is why it sounds so odd when Yoda moves the words around in the quote

@albiondumsday Womble or womble? ie proper noun or species?

above). This is not necessarily true of other languages: in Latin, *Julius videt Corneliam* and *Corneliam videt Julius* both mean the same ('Julius saw Cornelia'); you would have to change the endings of the two names to make it 'Cornelia saw Julius'. Other highly inflected languages such as German have a complex case structure and a huge number of word endings, as did Old English, which luckily for us we don't have to speak any more. Modern English only has a few inflections, such as the *-s* that changes *centipede* to *centipedes*, and the *-s*, *-ed* or *-ing* that changes *talk* to *talks*, *talked* or *talking*.

When the great cognitive linguist Steven Pinker writes in *The Language Instinct* that 'a preschooler's tacit knowledge of grammar is more sophisticated than the thickest style manual or the most state-of-the-art computer language system', he is not just having a pop at people like me who edit style manuals; he is saying that as children learn to speak a language, they quickly develop a sure grasp of its grammar and a feel for its patterns of usage. The mistakes they make reinforce this because they are normally based on trying to apply consistent rules to irregular ones, such as the perfectly logical 'we goed' rather than 'we went'. My one-year-old son's favourite TV programme, the surreally brilliant *In the Night Garden*, features a hero who communicates only in squeaks; the others only say their own names apart from Upsy Daisy, who can also say 'daisy doo' and 'pip-pip onk-onk'. (Chomsky would call this 'the poverty of the input'.) But listening to baby talk for a couple of years doesn't seem to stop children quickly learning how to use much more complex language. According to Chomsky, Universal Grammar, common to all languages, enables children to distil the syntactic patterns of the speech they hear. This view is so commonplace in every English language department in the world (and has been for decades), that it is amazing the majority of people have never heard of it.

If it's so simple, why are there so many grammar books? Why this one? The linguist David Crystal says in *Rediscover Grammar*: 'Everyone who speaks English *knows* grammar, intuitively and unconsciously. But not everyone who speaks English *knows about* grammar.' With hundreds of thousands of words to choose from (the OED lists over 615,000) and numerous ways to use them, it is hardly surprising that people make mistakes, or worry about making them. It's not that it's hard to communicate – however much or little formal education people have, they don't normally have problems making themselves understood to family, friends and colleagues. But the grammatical conventions we use when chatting to or texting people we know are not always suitable for talking, and particularly writing, in the wider world. It's perfectly reasonable to turn to books to help. Why some authors like to brand their readers as 'illiterate' for doing so is beyond me. I promise not to insult mine.

A word about Standard English. Many people assume this is related to the way posh people speak, but it is nothing to do with received pronunciation (RP) or any other accent: you can use Standard English if you have a northern England accent, as I do, or with a Scottish, Australian, Indian, Nigerian or any other accent, and whether you were taught Eton English or estuary English. Standard English is the variety of English used formally in such areas as education, politics, law, literature, the media and science. It is an internationally accepted way of writing the language. There are variations – for example, between American and British English spelling – but these

@speechmarks 'A thousand no's ...' Looks better that 'nos' but what's right and why?

are relatively small in the context of the language as a whole. An English speaker can read a story on a newspaper website in London, Los Angeles or Lagos without any difficulty. Imagine how much harder this would be if English spelling followed a particular variety of pronunciation. The grammar of written Standard English is broadly common to them all.

A standard language enables people to communicate beyond their immediate community with a nation, or world, of fellow speakers. Other languages have their equivalents: in French *le français standard*, in German *Hochdeutsch*, in Romanian *limba dacoromână*, in Chinese *Putonghua*. The grammar and vocabulary of Standard English are much the same everywhere they are found, from Manchester to Melbourne, from Massachusetts to Madras. Many grammar books fail to even mention this fact but when I say what I think is or isn't correct or appropriate, I will normally be referring to Standard English. And whether or not you speak with a posh accent has nothing to do with it.

The Sounds of Syntax

> *Grammar is not just a pain in the ass; it's the pole you grab to get your thoughts up on their feet and walking.*
> STEPHEN KING

> *We are almost ashamed to refer to the fact that a report has come to us that your brotherhood is teaching grammar to certain people.*
> POPE GREGORY THE GREAT (540–604)

@guardianstyle A thousand noes to 'no's' and 'nos'.

Syntax means sentence structure. In much the same way as my dad used to strip the car engine down, you can break a sentence into its constituent parts to see how it works. You can do the same with words, which is known as morphology – a word I had never come across until being asked, during an interview for a place on a master's degree in English at University College London (UCL), how 'interested in morphology' I was. 'Oh, very!'

Knowing how an engine works is not necessary to drive well, but a grasp of syntax can help you to communicate clearly, whether you are writing an essay, a love letter or a tweet. As with oxygen, you may not know much about it but syntax is everywhere: in *EastEnders* and Eminem, in a Nigella Lawson pudding recipe and a Seymore Butts porn movie, in Facebook status updates and in BBC Radio 5 Live football commentaries. In the Beatles' 'She Loves You'.

By the mid-1960s poor Lonnie Donegan had become distinctly uncool as beat groups like the Beatles, the Rolling Stones and the Who emerged to get me and my little moptopped mates twisting and shouting all through play-time. Half a century later, it is impossible to exaggerate the sheer thrill of listening to a record such as 'She Loves You' when it came out, given an extra frisson by older people's disapproval of the 'yeah, yeah, yeah' refrain, which they believed – wrongly as it turns out – would lead people of my generation to abandon the traditional spelling and pronunciation of the word 'yes'. (The grammar of the song is in fact immaculate, as you might have expected from its composers, two grammar-school boys.) Anyway, just as there's nothing you can sing that can't be sung, there's nothing about syntax

@JV8P As many as 70% of, or as much as 70% of?

that you can't learn by listening to pop music. As George Martin, the Beatles' producer, called his autobiography: *All You Need Is Ears*. So here's a playlist with a difference. It's an introduction to parts of speech, also known as word classes. But with a small nod towards Paul Simon, I'll call them the sounds of syntax.

'She Loves You'
THE BEATLES

'She loves you' is a neat little sentence that illustrates the point about word order in English, which is normally subject-verb-object (sometimes written SVO). Here *she* is the subject, *loves* is the verb, and *you* is the (direct) object. It can be paraphrased as who did what to whom. *She* is a pronoun: it stands in for a noun – 'she loves you' rather than 'Elsie loves you'. You don't need to know what a predicate is, but if you are wondering, it is what follows the subject, in this case 'loves you' (so: everything but the girl). Remember 'The Coffee Song'? It has a few extra bits, but the structure is the same: 'They' is the subject, '[ha]ve got' is the verb, 'an awful lot of coffee in Brazil' is the direct object.

A sentence is the main unit of expression in most languages, including English. If it makes sense, and has a main verb in it, it's a sentence. It can be a statement ('Dogs die in hot cars'), a question ('Do you believe in magic?'), an instruction ('Blame it on the boogie') or an exclamation ('Godspeed You, Black Emperor!').

From the top down, sentences comprise clauses, phrases and words. A clause is a group of words that usually contains a verb and its subject. A main clause can stand by itself as

---

@guardianstyle As much as 70% of the horsemeat was eaten by as many as 70% of the diners.

a sentence, like 'She loves you'; a subordinate clause has a verb in it, but cannot stand by itself, such as the italicised words in 'she loves you *when you buy her flowers*'. A phrase is a unit of one or more words, and there are several types: noun phrase, verb phrase, adverbial phrase, adjectival phrase and prepositional phrase. Phrases contain a head, the central element – so in the noun phrase 'a girl with red hair', *girl* is the head. As with a Russian doll, you can get phrases within phrases within phrases.

There are five basic types of a simple (one-clause) sentence:

- subject and verb ('David writes');
- subject, transitive verb, direct object ('Anna phoned the doctor');
- subject, transitive verb, indirect object, direct object ('David gave Alex advice');
- subject, copular verb, complement ('The baby is sleepy'); and
- subject, transitive verb, direct object, complement ('The members elected Nick treasurer').

A copular verb relates to states of being; the most common is 'to be'. A complement is so called because it completes the sentence. You can embellish these five types by adding on various bits and pieces, but 'Blue-eyed journalist and author *David* regularly *gave* young *Alex* some unwanted *advice* via email, text message and carrier pigeon' is still the same basic sentence with a few extra phrases thrown in.

Sentences comprising more than one main clause joined by a conjunction or semicolon ('She loves you but not as much as I do') are known as compound sentences. Complex sentences are those consisting of a main clause plus subordinate clause or clauses, such as a conditional clause ('She'll love you if you buy her a diamond ring') or a relative clause ('She loves you, which you know is jolly good').

A sentence can be short.

A process of ellipsis (not, in this case, three dots ... but similar in that it implies something has been left out) enables us to make sense of very brief statements, the omitted words being supplied from what is understood or has been said before:

Wayne: *No way!*
Garth: *Way!* (Or, for emphasis: *Yes way!*)

These are both sentences. We infer something like (ellipsis in square brackets):

Wayne: *[There is] no way [that can be so]!*
Garth: *[On the contrary, there is a] way!*

With the help of the Beatles and *Wayne's World*, we have just covered most of the basics of syntax in two minutes and 21 seconds. Yeah, yeah, yeah, yeah.

'Me Myself and I'
DE LA SOUL

As we have seen, pronouns are used in place of a noun. Do you really want to know all the different types? Here they are anyway, with an example of each:

@guardianstyle Log in or log on with your login or logon.

- personal (*you*);
- possessive (*your, yours*);
- demonstrative (*these*);
- relative (*whose*);
- interrogative (*what*);
- indefinite (*something*);
- reflexive (*myself*); and
- reciprocal (*each other*).

Another way of doing it:

- subject pronouns (*I, you, he, she, it, we, they*);
- object pronouns (*me, you, him, her, it, us, them*);
- possessive pronouns (*my, your, his, her, its, our, their*, and *mine, yours, his, hers, its, ours, theirs*); and
- relative pronouns (*that, which, who, whom*).

Personal pronouns can function as the subject or object of a sentence, leading to a common problem: should the Queen say 'my husband and I' or 'my husband and me'? Either. In '*My husband and I* love horseracing' the italicised phrase is the subject. In 'The horse was a gift to *my husband and me*' it is the object. If in doubt, try the singular: 'I love horseracing'; 'it was a gift to me'. Another issue that vexes people is when to use 'myself'. I will come to that, as well as some thoughts on how to be a good feminist when English lacks a gender-neutral third-person singular pronoun.

But first, stop reading, take a break and watch the superb video of 'Me Myself and I' on YouTube. It's set in a classroom and De La Soul (a trio) have great fun playing on the fact that the title might refer to three people or one.

@ClareKirkp Is 'pre-planning' a tautology or not?

'Every Little Thing She Does Is Magic'
THE POLICE

Although the subject of a sentence will typically be a noun or pronoun, it doesn't have to be. In this case, the subject is a clause, *Every little thing she does*; the verb, obviously, is *is* and *magic* is the complement of the verb. A complement can be an adjective or noun: she was *delighted* when they appointed her *editor*.

'Blood Sugar Sex Magik'
RED HOT CHILI PEPPERS

Flea, blood, sugar, sex, magik, Los Angeles.

No, not a Rorschach inkblot test or the programme for an unusual adventure holiday. These are all nouns, traditionally defined as people, places or things – a definition scorned by linguists, but which most people nonetheless find useful. But even if a noun is just one word, it is also helpful to think of it as a noun phrase because it can be expanded: blood, for example, can become 'all this red blood'. The same applies to other types of phrase. A noun phrase, as we saw earlier, can be the subject of a sentence, a direct object, an indirect object or a complement.

Many words fit into more than one word class. Sex, for example, can take the form of a noun, as in the title here; a verb, as in I Wanna Sex You Up; or an adjective, Get Up (I Feel Like Being a Sex Machine). And that is before taking into account closely related words: Sexual Healing, Do Ya Think I'm Sexy, Sex-O-Matic Venus Freak, and many more. Don't say syntax isn't sexy.

@guardianstyle We've pre-decided that one: it is.

Red Hot Chili Peppers, unlike the Police, favour the Middle English spelling:

> *He kepte his pacient a ful greet deel*
> *In houres by his magik natureel.*
> CHAUCER, *PROLOGUE TO THE CANTERBURY TALES*

'The Sound of Silence'
SIMON & GARFUNKEL

Determiners – an uninspiring name – are so called because they are said to 'determine' the noun. Whatever that means. The most common and best known are *a*, the indefinite article, and *the*, the definite article. You definitely know whether it's definite or indefinite: 'the dog has bitten my leg' is a dog people know about or which you have already referred to; 'a dog has bitten my leg' could be any old dog. The difference can be quite subtle, however. 'The sound of silence' is an oxymoron, an apparent contradiction, but by choosing the definite article Paul Simon gave the phrase a specific impact that the vaguer 'a sound of silence' would have lacked.

Central determiners are *any*, *each*, *every*, *some*, *this*, *that*. Note that they can be used in place of *a* or *the* to change the focus: 'this dog has bitten my leg', 'oh, THAT sound of silence!', 'every cake you bake, I'll be watching you'. Predeterminers such as *all* go before the central ones, and postdeterminers such as *last* go after. So to return to the noun phrase 'all this red blood', *all* is a predeterminer and *this* is a central determiner; in the noun phrase 'the last time', *the* is of course the central determiner and *last* a postdeterminer.

@lisapr1ce Is it skill set, skill-set or skillset?

'Wake Up and Make Love with Me'
IAN DURY AND THE BLOCKHEADS
Wake up, make love, eat, shoot, leave, imagine.

These are all verbs. At school we were told verbs are 'doing' words. As they don't always do all that much, they are also known as 'actions and states'. If a sentence or clause hasn't got a verb, it isn't a sentence or clause, whatever it may claim.

If anyone mentions 'strong' verbs, they mean irregular verbs, like *be* (I am, you are, he is, they were, and so on), as opposed to 'weak' verbs, which are regular, like *love* (I love, you love, he loves, she loved, and so on).

Verbs raise various issues that I deal with in detail (but don't be alarmed: not too much detail) elsewhere. The infinitive is the bare, uninflected form of the verb: eat, shoot, leave. The *to* is called a particle: 'I love to eat leaves.' Feel free to insert anything you like, within reason, between the particle and the infinitive.

A participle is an adjectival form of the verb: the present participle ends in *-ing* (learning, burning, seeing) and the past in *-ed*, *-t* or *-n* (learned, burnt, seen). In 'Alfred burned the cakes; the cakes were burnt' *burned* is the past tense, describing what Alfred did; *burnt* is the past participle, describing what state the cakes were in as a result. In the sentence, 'Burning with rage, Blackadder and Baldrick are burning Johnson's dictionary', the first *burning* is a present participle (what state Blackadder and Baldrick are in) and the second is a form of the present tense (what they are doing).

As with noun phrases, verb phrases can be one word (*burned*) or expanded by adding auxiliary verbs – the four words in italics here comprise a verb phrase: 'The cakes *must have been burned* by Alfred.'

'I Got You (I Feel Good)'
JAMES BROWN

Adjectives 'modify' nouns by giving information about them. They come in two groups: descriptive, like *tall*, *dark* or *handsome*, and classifying, such as *green* or *Russian*, and they come in that order: a *dark green* door, a *handsome Russian* president. You don't need a comma or 'and' if they are different types, but you do if they are the same type: 'a *tall, handsome* man'. They are said to be attributive if they come before the noun (a *handsome* man) or predicative if they come after (a man who was *handsome*).

Mark Twain, who had a lot to say about language, mostly sensible, did not much like adjectives, advising: 'When you catch an adjective, kill it. No, I don't mean utterly, but kill most of them – then the rest will be valuable. An adjective habit … is as hard to get rid of as any other vice.' Journalists are told to avoid adjectives that get in the way of fair reporting, such as 'controversial', which typically means the writer disapproves of something ('the government's controversial plans … ').

Purists might object to James Brown's 'I feel good – I knew that I would' on the grounds that the adjective 'good' should strictly be the adverb 'well'. Not only have such people got no soul, but they are also wrong. There's a credible case for 'I feel good' because *feel* is a copular verb, which as I mentioned refers to states of being – most obviously *be*, but also *act*, *appear*, *seem*, and similar. As we have seen, copular verbs

---

@Gbeecham 'Fine-tooth comb' or 'fine tooth-comb?'

can take an adjective as complement ('the baby is *sleepy*'). And *good*, my friends, is an adjective. Which is why 'I act good' (adjective – I pretend to be good) means something quite different from 'I act well' (adverb – I'm a good actor). Anyway, James Brown was cool and if he felt good, it's fine by me. Other of his songs include 'Hot (I Need to Be Loved, Loved, Loved, Loved)' and 'I Got Ants in My Pants (And I Want to Dance)', suggesting that if there is a volume two of this playlist, or this book, it might well be devoted to the Godfather of Soul.

'I Only Have Eyes for You'
THE FLAMINGOS

Adverbs modify verbs, adjectives or other adverbs to describe such things as how, when, where, how often, how far and to what extent. They often end in -*ly* – *sadly, madly, dangerously, frequently* – but they don't have to: *abroad, behind, yesterday, quite, very* and *to the end of time* are all adverbs.

It may not surprise you to learn that Twain didn't like adverbs any more than adjectives: 'Substitute *damn* every time you're inclined to write *very*,' he advised. 'Your editor will delete it and the writing will be just as it should be.'

It's certainly, undoubtedly, very easy indeed to overdo adverbs. This clumsy sentence, in an article about F Scott Fitzgerald's *The Great Gatsby*, appeared in the *Guardian* in May 2013 (I have italicised the adverbs): '*Almost* 90 years later, Gatsby is *regularly* named one of the greatest novels *ever* written in English, and has *annually* sold millions of copies *globally*.' If I had got my hands on this, I would have rewritten it thus: 'Almost 90 years later, Gatsby is regularly named one of the greatest novels in English, and sells millions of copies a year all over the world.'

In Noël Coward's *Hay Fever*, there is a parlour game called 'In the Manner of the Word', in which one person has to guess the adverb being acted out by the rest of the team: 'winsomely' turns out to be quite tricky. Such adverbs are frowned on these days. Creative writing courses say 'show, don't tell' and when you look at examples from the heyday of the adverb, you can see why. The following all appear within two pages of Agatha Christie's *Hercule Poirot's Christmas* (1938): 'Alfred said warmly … David said vaguely … George said sharply … Lydia said sharply … Hilda said firmly … Lydia said to Hilda privately … Hilda said thoughtfully … Hilda said thoughtfully [again] … She added musingly … ' I read 230 pages of this wearily.

Adverbs can be grouped into various categories, such as degree (I *entirely* agree), place (I will go *abroad*), time (I want it *now*), and manner (she gestured *vaguely*). Adverbs of degree can be further subdivided into emphasising (*really*), intensifying (*immensely*), moderating (*rather*), and focusing (*only*). This may be of interest if you like making lists of things. The other category is sentence adverbs, which govern the whole sentence, as in 'Hopefully, we will reach the summit'. Some traditionalists still maintain that this is wrong because *hopefully* is also a manner adverb, as in 'We set off hopefully for the summit'. The suggestion is that the clunky 'It is to be hoped that we will reach the summit' is more correct. Unfortunately, this view is sadly mistaken. Thankfully, many of us happily await the day when such people finally notice that many adverbs can be used to govern the whole sentence or just the verb: *unfortunately*, *sadly*, *thankfully*, *happily* – and *hopefully*. Even the normally sensible Robert Allen, in *How to Write Better English*, says *hopefully* 'is best reserved for spoken use, and should be avoided in more formal writing, if only to avoid causing irritation to language purists who might be reading'. Hopefully, you will agree with me that they deserve all the irritation they get.

Some armchair grammarians also get worked up about the position of focusing adverbs, suggesting for example that 'I Only Have Eyes for You' should have been written 'I Have Eyes for Only You'. HW Fowler called such people 'those friends from whom the English language may well pray to be saved'. In such cases, any sensible person would know the meaning at once from the context. But where you place the adverb can sometimes make a difference. Compare:

- 'Rubbing it with a dock leaf will only ease the pain.' (It won't cure it.)
- 'Only rubbing it with a dock leaf will ease the pain.' (Nothing else will do.)

Some adverbs raise more questions than they answer and, while they are fine in speech, should be avoided in writing. If you see any of the following examples in a newspaper, alarm bells should be ringing: *apparently* (to whom?), *evidently* (what evidence?), *reportedly* (reported by whom?).

Note *fast* is an adjective in 'he is a fast runner' and an adverb in 'he ran fast'. You can see this from the opposites: 'he is a slow runner' and 'he ran slowly'.

@guardianstyle Well it's not Latin, for a start.

The best thing about adverbs is that, if you don't know what something is, you can always bluff by saying it's an adverb. The man who taught me the 'when in doubt, it's an adverb' rule is now a professor. To finish this section with a cartoon from *Private Eye*, by Roger Latham:

'Tell me this: when you say "fantastic" and "incredibly" do you simply mean "good" and "very"?'
'Absolutely!'

'My Head Is My Only House Unless it Rains'
CAPTAIN BEEFHEART AND THE MAGIC BAND

Conjunctions are linking words. The obvious ones are *and*, *but* and *or*, but there are lots of words that can be used to conjoin two things, hence the name.

Coordinating conjunctions, most commonly *and* and *but*, link two clauses of equal status. In the Ian Dury song discussed above: the two main clauses 'Wake up' and 'make love with me' are coordinated by the conjunction *and*. Note that you could leave it out and have two sentences that both stand alone and make perfect sense: 'Wake up'; 'Make love with me.' They are not very polite, though. The mnemonic FANBOYS has been recommended as a way to remember the coordinating conjunctions: *for, and, nor, but, or, yet, so*.

Subordinating conjunctions link a main clause to a subordinate clause. Typical examples are *because*, *whether* and *unless*, as here: the main clause 'My Head Is My Only House' is linked to the subordinate clause 'it rains' by the conjunction *unless*. You could argue that the two clauses could stand alone, and are therefore of equal status, but that's stretching things for 'it rains'. And if Captain Beefheart, the great Don Van Vliet, had written 'unless it's raining', one of the greatest of all love songs would have lost some of its poetry.

Other words that can be used as subordinating conjunctions are *after, although, as, before, if, since, than, though, until, when* and *while*. Note that these can all take on other roles. For instance, *than* can be used as a preposition ('he is even dafter than me'), but as a conjunction it is 'he is even dafter than I am', because now *than* is joining two clauses.

Correlative conjunctions include *both ... and*; *either ... or*; and *not only ... but also*. The important thing here is to be consistent and finish what you start. It's very annoying to read 'not only' and discover much later that there is not going to be a 'but also' to tidy things up nicely.

You may well have been taught at school never to begin a sentence with a conjunction, particularly not *and* or *but*. I was. But luckily I discovered that it is nothing more than a silly superstition. More about this in the next chapter.

'(They Long to Be) Close to You'
THE CARPENTERS

Prepositions are little words such as *at, for, in, after, from, to, among* and *between* that show the relationship between other words in a sentence. They can be short phrases, such as *close to* you or *on top of* the world. They always take an object: 'from *me* to *you*'. Hence 'between you and me', not 'between you and I'; 'to us Conservatives', not 'to we Conservatives'.

An understanding of syntax makes thorny questions straightforward. For example, why is it stay awhile, but stay for a while? Once you recognise *awhile* as an adverb, and *a while* as a noun phrase equivalent to 'a period of time', used as an object and governed by the preposition *for*, it's simple.

Choosing the right preposition can, however, be tricky: you can be absorbed *in* a task, but water is absorbed *by* a sponge, you are forbidden *to* but prohibited *from*. Sometimes they are missed out altogether, as in 'they protested the verdict', which I wish to protest against very strongly.

'There's a Guy Works Down the Chip Shop Swears He's Elvis'

KIRSTY MACCOLL

This song title is a sentence that contains four noun phrases (*a guy*, *the chip shop*, *he*, *Elvis*), four verb phrases (*[there]'s*, *works*, *swears*, *[he]'s*), and a prepositional phrase (*down the chip shop*) that in turn contains one of the noun phrases (*the chip shop*), which in turn contains the adjectival phrase (*chip*). All this and an example of something called 'existential there' (*There's*). Oh, and there are two relative clauses (*works down the chip shop*, *swears he's Elvis*). Plus a couple of determiners. And possibly some parts that I've missed. I mention all this just to illustrate that the more you get into phrase-structure grammar, the more fun you can have.

It's a great title for a great song, despite all this grammar – or perhaps because of it: the syntax reflects the fact that even if the language is colloquial, the structure is sophisticated. Now just think what you could do with *My People Were Fair and Had Sky in Their Hair ... But Now They're Content to Wear Stars on Their Brows*, the title of the debut album by Marc Bolan's Tyrannosaurus Rex, which comprises two main clauses, each of which contains two further clauses.

Incidentally, if you are ever stuck for a funny headline or a bit of wordplay on the theme of JRR Tolkien, I recommend: 'There's a guy works down the chip shop swears he's Elvish.'

'Wow'
KATE BUSH (or, if you prefer, Kylie Minogue with the same title, different song)
Oops!, OMG!, Phew! and the like are known as interjections. Old novels would sometimes use the verb 'ejaculate' with interjections, as in: *'Oops!' he ejaculated.* My mates and I found this hilarious at school.

Would you believe that I have actually created this playlist on my iPod? Of course. Because that, as some readers will be all too aware, is the kind of thing a nerd does.

Pass Notes: Berks and Wankers

Not the coalition government again. This is about grammar, not politics. And I'll do the jokes.

Sorry. Age? The distinction was first made in *The King's English* by Kingsley Amis, published posthumously in 1997.

Appearance? 'Berks are careless, coarse, crass, gross and of what anybody would agree is a lower social class than one's own ... '

I didn't come here to be insulted. 'They speak in a slip-shod way with dropped Hs, intruded glottal stops and many mistakes in grammar. Left to them the English language would die of impurity, like Latin.'

And wankers? 'Wankers are prissy, fussy, priggish, prim and of what they would probably misrepresent as a higher social class than one's own. They speak in an over-precise way with much pedantic insistence on letters not generally sounded, especially Hs. Left to them the language would die of purity, like medieval Latin.'

Why are we discussing this now? The author of this book thinks it's an amusing way to raise the issue of how grammar tends to divide people into opposing groups: traditionalists and modernists, prescriptivists and descriptivists, for example.

Any examples that aren't libellous? Well, by Amis's definition someone who thinks the song should be *I Have Eyes for Only You* would be a wanker. Whereas a berk would be someone who says things like 'protested the verdict'.

Can someone be both a berk and a wanker? As I said, this is about grammar, not politicians. In fact Amis conceded that most people are neither berks nor wankers, but 'try to pursue a course between the slipshod and the punctilious'.

Here's some grammar for you. Do you realise that the collective noun is a wunch of bankers? I said I'll do the jokes.

@markturner Osborne said 'one pence' off a pint

Do say: 'Everyone has always regarded any usage but his own as either barbarous or pedantic.' (Evelyn Waugh)

Don't say: To be honest, I preferred *Lucky Jim*.

The Pedants' Revolt

> *I do here in the Name of all the Learned and Polite*
> *Persons of the Nation, complain to your Lordship, as*
> *First Minister, that our Language is extremely imperfect;*
> *that its daily Improvements are by no means in*
> *proportion to its daily Corruptions; and the Pretenders*
> *to polish and refine it, have chiefly multiplied Abuses*
> *and Absurdities; and, that in many Instances, it offends*
> *against every Part of Grammar.*
>
> JONATHAN SWIFT, 'A PROPOSAL FOR CORRECTING, IMPROVING AND
> ASCERTAINING THE ENGLISH TONGUE' (1712)

The great grammarian Otto Jesperson, writing in 1909, said English grammar was 'not ... a set of stiff dogmatic precepts, according to which some things are correct and others absolutely wrong'; but it was living and developing, 'founded on the past' but preparing the way for the future, 'something that is not always consistent or perfect, but progressing and perfectible – in one word, human'. Language has been changing since the Tower of Babel and will continue to do so. The most conservative of traditionalists admit this, and claim to accept it, though they are oddly shy about putting forward examples of change they are happy with. Just think

@guardianstyle Not just economically illiterate, then.

for a moment about technological change and how it drives language. Some of us can remember when Spam was a sort of cheap ham they made into fritters for our school dinners. Happy days.

A lot of people seem to think all change must be for the worse. Such fears, as relating to language, date from at least the 18th century. Usage, particularly spelling, had been fluid until then: a law passed in Elizabeth I's reign used the alternative spellings *briberie* and *briberye* in the same sentence and Shakespeare was, to say the least, relaxed about how to spell words (including his own name). Samuel Johnson and others sought to bring some order to the chaos. Johnson produced his dictionary in 1755 (to replace the one, you may remember, burned by Blackadder and Baldrick). The two most important grammar books of the period, by Lindley Murray in 1795 and Robert Lowth in 1862, had a huge influence until well into the 20th century. These are the men you can thank for such 'rules' as not splitting infinitives. The OED, which started to appear in sections from 1888, was a big step towards settling things. The grammarians, notably HW Fowler with his *Dictionary of Modern English Usage* (1926), continued that process. By the time I started at school, in the 1950s, English teachers had a very firm idea of exactly what was and wasn't right. Even when they were wrong.

This brings me to the descriptive v prescriptive argument. For at least 50 years almost all academic linguistics has been descriptive, concerning itself with how language is structured and used without passing judgment on what is right or wrong.

Lexicographers, similarly, work by establishing that a word is in use with a particular meaning. If it does, they will

@Abridgwater Chancellor or chancellor?

put it in the dictionary and ignore the howls of protest from those who think this is providing respectable cover for the barbarians who want to wreck our beautiful language. Does this mean that things are getting worse? Lynne Truss, who wrote a book about punctuation, typified such fears when she referred to 'the justifiable despair of the well educated in a dismally illiterate world'. According to this argument, it all started to go wrong in the 1970s 'when teachers upheld the view that grammar and spelling got in the way of self-expression'. Jonathan Swift expressed similar concerns 300 years ago. Conservatives long for a golden age, usually about 50 years in the past, when everyone knew their grammar and all was right with the world.

Sadly, however, there never was a golden age. In his autobiography, the late actor Dirk Bogarde, who was privately educated, describes his astonishment when he joined the army in the 1940s on finding that all the men in his platoon, who were state educated, were in effect illiterate. Yet this was the era when, according to Truss, most people did 'know how to write'. I attended a grammar school as one of the top 10 per cent or so who passed the 11-plus. Even among this elite, many took little interest in English grammar and even those who did had forgotten most of it by the time they got to university.

In May 2013, a 'bad grammar' award was given to an open letter published by academic opponents of the Conservative education secretary, Michael Gove. It is characteristic of such awards that the judges described as 'simply illiterate' the following sentences: 'Much of it demands too much too young ... Little account is taken of children's potential interests and

---

@guardianstyle He may be an upper-class twit, but like all chancellors he's lowercase to us.

capacities, or that young children need to relate abstract ideas to their experience, lives and activity.' While it's true that the latter sentence would have read better if 'the fact' had been inserted before 'that young children', if this really is 'the worst use of English over the last 12 months by people who should know better', as the judges ruled, it suggests that they were making a political, rather than a grammatical, point. One judge in particular, a man who advocates teaching Latin by rote to three-year-olds, objected to the phrase 'too much too young', which he appeared not to have come across. It was a No 1 hit for the Specials in 1980. A passing fad, perhaps.

For their part, academics have a pretty poor record of explaining descriptive linguistics to the public, and can come across as aloof and arrogant. (There are exceptions, some of whom are quoted in this book and appear in the bibliography.) Can there ever be peace, when the two sides are so entrenched? Or must they for ever be in conflict, like the farmer and the cowman in *Oklahoma!*? I'd like to think there is a middle way that doesn't condemn but does help people to gain confidence in their use of language. I am not arguing that everything is perfect; far from it, as you are about to discover. But there's no sound evidence that standards are worse than when Lynne Truss and I were at school. And rather than blame it all on teachers and the national curriculum, the why-oh-why-are-things-so-awful-it-was-so-much-better-in-my-day lobby might wonder why it is that many of the worst language abuses come from people who have actually been well (often expensively) educated: politicians, business people, civil servants, marketing executives, and others. As we shall see.

CHAPTER 2

The Rules Do Not Apply

A dozen things people worry about unnecessarily

When is misuse not misuse? When everybody does it.

STEVEN PINKER, *THE LANGUAGE INSTINCT*

A Grammar book does not attempt to teach people how they ought to speak, but on the contrary, unless it is a very bad or a very old work, it merely states how, as a matter of fact, certain people do speak at the time at which it is written.

HC WYLD, *ELEMENTARY LESSONS IN ENGLISH GRAMMAR* (1925)

'Rules', declared Desmond McDonald – fiercely stirring jam into his rice pudding to make it look like blood – 'are made for fools.' You probably won't know Desmond. He was my first role model, aged five: to good little boys like me, his frequent challenges to authority inspired fear and envy in equal measure. One day he put his disdain for the norms of infant school behaviour into practice by leading a noisy, chaotic charge of about half a dozen of us along the corridor outside the headmistress's office, an offence we knew would lead to a caning, which it duly did. (It was legal to assault five-year-olds with a big stick in 1958.)

This painful episode may be one reason why I have been inclined to play things by the rules ever since. And as we have seen, people tend to think of grammar as a list of strict rules that they deviate from at their peril. But some traditional grammatical rules hinder, rather than help, communication. Prescriptions can be useful, but only if they help you get better; you don't take medicine just for the sake of it. Desmond McDonald had a point.

To Infinitive and Beyond

In those days men were real men, women were real women, small furry creatures from Alpha Centauri were real small furry creatures from Alpha Centauri. And all dared to brave unknown terrors, to do mighty deeds, to boldly split infinitives that no man had split before.

DOUGLAS ADAMS, *THE HITCHHIKER'S GUIDE TO THE GALAXY*

Would you convey my compliments to the purist who reads your proofs and tell him or her that I write in a sort of broken-down patois which is something like the way a Swiss waiter talks, and that when I split an infinitive, God damn it, I split it so it will stay split.

RAYMOND CHANDLER IN A LETTER TO HIS PUBLISHER

Geoffrey K Pullum, a scarily erudite Scottish linguistics professor – and, unless this is an internet hoax, a keyboard player in the 1960s with Geno Washington & the Ram Jam Band – calls them 'zombie rules: though dead, they shamble mindlessly on … they eat your brain'. And none more so than the 'rule' that the particle *to* and the infinitive form of

@Sadgrovem Instore, in-store or in store (as in Sale Instore). Which is English?

the verb should not be separated, as they are in Star Trek's eloquent mission statement 'to boldly go where no man has gone before', a phrase that echoes Byron's 'to slowly trace the forest's shady scene' and inspired the following headline I wrote, perhaps less eloquently, on an *Independent* piece about hair replacement: 'To baldly grow where no mane has gone before.'

Stubbornly to resist splitting infinitives can sound awkward and pompous ('the economic precipice on which they claim perpetually to be poised') or, worse, ambiguous: 'He offered personally to guarantee the loan that the Clintons needed to buy their house' makes it unclear whether the offer, or the guarantee, was personal.

Pullum quotes a report in the *Economist* saying the Russian parliament was 'considering a bill that would force any NGO receiving cash from abroad publicly to label itself a "foreign agent".' Does this mean NGOs receiving cash from abroad in public, or having to label themselves in public? *Economist* readers just had to guess; but if it means the latter, it needs to say 'to publicly label' or 'to label itself publicly'. Now the *Economist* is a justifiably respected news magazine, better written and edited than most of its British counterparts, so you might well wonder what hope there is for the rest of us.

The non-existent 'rule' to leave adverbs staggering haplessly around the sentence like the odd toddler out in a game of musical chairs is not just half baked: it's fully baked, with a fried egg and slice of pineapple on top. But it's remarkably persistent, particularly among people who have been well educated (but not, clearly, as well as they think). In his 2013 budget George Osborne, the chancellor of the exchequer, announced: 'My message to those who make a living advising other people how aggressively to avoid their taxes is this: this government is not going to let you get away with it.' I think he meant that the advice was about aggressively avoiding taxes, rather than how aggressively to do so, but 'how aggressively to avoid' is as ambiguous as it is clunky.

Distinguished *Guardian* commentators are by no means immune from this kind of thing: 'The challenge for Ed Miliband is how to capture the right tone of indignation at this injustice and class bias, how witheringly to crush the wilful ignorance of Tory backbenchers … ' This sentence might mean one of two things: the challenge for Ed Miliband is how witheringly he should crush the wilfully ignorant Tories – a lot, or a little bit? – or how best to crush them witheringly. Knowing the writer, she probably means the latter – in which case, why not say so? 'The challenge for Ed Miliband is how to capture the right tone of indignation at this injustice and class bias, how to witheringly crush the wilful ignorance of Tory backbenchers … ' does the job neatly and unambiguously.

It's common sense to put adverbs where they are most natural and clear, and that's often immediately after the *to*: to boldly go, to publicly label, to aggressively avoid, to witheringly crush. Sometimes writers are so desperate to avoid doing the splits that they don't notice they would be better off leaving out the adverb altogether – as in *Eats, Shoots & Leaves* where Lynne Truss tells us 'you may find it within you not only to tolerate these exceptions but positively to treasure them', without explaining how you could treasure something other than in a positive way.

@eseesea Helter skelter, helter-skelter or helterskelter?

Following a 'rule' that confuses the reader is barmy. The last word on the subject goes to George Bernard Shaw who, after an editor tinkered with his infinitives, declared: 'I don't care if he is made to go quickly, or to quickly go – but go he must!'

Unsplitting the infinitive
Irritation factor: 9/10
Frequency of error: 8/10
Misused by: too many professional writers who ought
  to know better

Typical example:

He was never ashamed publicly to bear witness.

PETER CAREY, *OSCAR AND LUCINDA*
(WINNER OF THE BOOKER PRIZE, 1988)

The Things One Has to Put Up with

*Daddy, what did you bring that book that I don't want
to be read to out of up for?*

SENTENCE ENDING IN FIVE PREPOSITIONS, QUOTED BY STEVEN PINKER

Prepositions relate one word or phrase to another to express place (*to* the office, *in* the net, *over* the rainbow) or time (*before* the flood, *after* the goldrush). Other prepositions include *between, on, under, near, behind, by, in front of, along with, out of, because of, by means of, in charge of, in*

@guardianstyle helter-skelter: fairground,
Helter Skelter: White Album.

accordance with. They are followed by an object: with love from *me* to *you*.

In the 17th century the writer John Dryden, suddenly deciding that ending a sentence with a preposition was 'not elegant' because you couldn't do it in Latin, set about ruining some of his best prose by rewriting it so that 'the end he aimed at' became 'the end at which he aimed', and so on. Like not splitting the infinitive, this became a 'rule' when taught by grammarians influenced by Latin.

Did Winston Churchill satirise this by saying 'that is the type of pedantry up with which I shall not put'? Most books on this subject assert that he did, but he probably didn't, although it did appear (anonymously) in *Strand Magazine*, to which Churchill was a contributor, in 1942. This helps explain why the quote appears in so many different forms. HW Fowler had put it much better in *Modern English Usage* a few years earlier: 'The power of saying ... *People worth talking to* instead of *People with whom it is worth while to talk* is not one to be lightly surrendered.'

Not only is there no rule about where to put prepositions, but there is also no rule about how to choose the right one: you just have to learn, for example, that it's *forbidden to* but *prohibited from*. One of the things I get most complaints from readers about is when the paper omits them after *appeal* and *protest* (as in 'appeal the sentence', 'protest the verdict'). There's nothing wrong with this in American English but it makes many users of British English, including me, shudder; so here's a heartfelt appeal – it's 'appeal against' and 'protest against' or 'protest over', please.

@DuncanNRoss Arse over tit, or arse-over-tit?

Prepositions fall out of fashion, for instance 'telephone to', which to judge by old novels people stopped using some time in the 1960s. Although not Alan Bennett, who was writing 'telephone to' in the *London Review of Books* as recently as January 2013. I'd telephone to him to point this out if I had his number.

Don't Get in a Bad Mood over the Subjunctive

The subjunctive mood is in its death throes, and the best thing to do is put it out of its misery as soon as possible.
W SOMERSET MAUGHAM

Damn the subjunctive!
MARK TWAIN

The subjunctive is a verb form (technically, 'mood') expressing hypothesis, typically to indicate that something is being demanded, proposed, imagined or insisted: 'he demanded that she resign', 'she insisted Jane sit down', and so on. You can spot it in the third person singular of the present tense (*resign*, *sit down* instead of *resigns*, *sits*) and in the forms *be* and *were* of the verb *to be*: if I were [not was] you, I'd tell the truth; if she were [not was] honest, she would quit; I demand that the editor meet [not meets] my aspirations; it's vital that she pay [not pays] the mortgage.

Maugham, who wrote the words quoted above in 1949, might be surprised to see my son Freddie's bookshelf, which contains *If I Were a Pig* ... (Jellycat Books, 2008), a

---

@guardianstyle He went arse over tit.
It was an arse-over-tit moment.

companion volume to *If I Were a Dinosaur* ... and *If I Were a Duck* ... The subjunctive, far from dying, may even be making a modest comeback: in an academic paper entitled 'The Use of the Subjunctive in Re-membering [sic] Conversations with Those Who are Grieving', it was argued that use of the subjunctive 'can be valuable in the scaffolding of sustaining narratives' for people who have been bereaved because it helps to validate their sense that a loved one who has died retains a presence, often very vivid, in their lives.

It's much more common in American than British English, and often found in formal or poetic contexts – in the song 'If I Were a Rich Man' from the musical *Fiddler on the Roof*, for example. The Orange Crate Art blog notes that the subjunctive is appropriate when 'stating conditions that are contrary to fact', contrasting Tim Hardin's lovely song lyric 'If I were a carpenter, would you marry me anyway?' with the distinctly more prosaic 'If I train as a carpenter, I will get to wear safety goggles.' It's not true, however, that David and Don Was came under pressure from language purists to change the name of their band to Were (Not Was).

You might argue that the subjunctive adds elegance to formal writing, as in this sentence by my colleague Gary Younge: 'It was as though Charlie Brown's teacher were standing for leader of the opposition.' The meaning would be just as clear if he had written 'was standing for leader of the opposition', but I think his use of the subjunctive is pleasing, especially when compared with an example of a leader writer who didn't use it: 'If every election or ballot in which there are cases of bad practice was to be invalidated, democracy would soon become a laughing stock.' No one died and no

---

@TheRealJoeCox When did 'gotten' become a word?

great harm was done, but professional writers should at least be aware of the distinction.

In another example, Adrian Searle writes of a new portrait of the Duchess of Cambridge: 'Were it a photograph, it would be the sort that hangs in a high street photographer's window as a testament to the wonders of digital improvement ... Were it a portrait of anyone else, it would be of no interest whatsoever.' I reckon 'if it was a photograph' and 'if it was a portrait of anyone else' sound prosaic in comparison.

The point, however, is that when it comes to the subjunctive, it's entirely up to you. There are usually ways round it: for example, 'he demanded her resignation' and, of course, 'if I was' (which doesn't seem to have done Midge Ure any harm: 'If I was a soldier...'). I don't know if the journalist Simon Heffer is a fan of Midge, but he's certainly a fan of the subjunctive, recommending such usages as 'if I be wrong, I shall be defeated' and 'though you be old, you are handsome'. So be it – if you want to sound like a country bumpkin or pirate.

When I was growing up in the north of England you quite often heard people use 'were' for 'was' (as in 'I were going down the road last night'), so when Lady Chatterley seeks out Mellors the day after they first make love 'to see if it were really real' I think this is DH Lawrence's dialect rather than an attempt to make the subjunctive sexy.

English grammar invariably offers an escape route to people who regard the subjunctive as old-fashioned. So using 'if he was to become famous' instead of the subjunctive choices – 'were he to become famous' or 'if he were to become famous' – is unlikely to upset anyone. Apart from

@guardianstyle At least 1,000 years ago in Old English. And it still is, in US English.

Simon Heffer. Note, however, that you can't say 'was he to become famous' unless as a question.

The most important thing is that, as with the misuse of *whom* instead of *who*, using the subjunctive wrongly is worse than not using it at all. Many novelists randomly scatter 'weres' about their pages as if 'was' were – or, indeed, was – going out of fashion. Back in 1926, HW Fowler's *Modern English Usage* noted that while the subjunctive was found in formal writing or speech, it was 'seldom obligatory'. So unless you are writing songs or poetry, or learning a foreign language, you don't really need to worry about it. As it were.

Incidentally, most grammar books say 'God save the Queen' is an example of the subjunctive but surely it is an appeal to God to save the Queen, rather than an assertion that God is saving her, and therefore no more subjunctive than the Beatles singing 'please please me'.

Serial Offenders

> *Who gives a fuck about an Oxford comma?*
> VAMPIRE WEEKEND

Quite a few people, it turns out, especially in the US. The horrified reaction to a claim on Twitter in 2011 that 'Oxford University is abandoning the Oxford comma' came chiefly from Americans alarmed at this new threat to the special relationship. The fact that it wasn't true did little to calm them. This is unsurprising, as the *Chicago Manual of Style* regards the Oxford (or serial) comma – the last in a list, immediately

@Tmorgoeva Why is it called hat-trick?

before the word 'and' – as mandatory: 'When a conjunction joins the last two elements in a series of three or more, a comma – known as the serial or series comma or the Oxford comma – should appear.' To true believers in this maxim, a flag that you or I might regard as red, white and blue is in fact red, white, and blue. The rule has the potential to introduce enough unnecessary pauses to your prose to make your Christmas card list read like something by Harold Pinter.

The furore led many people to assume that Oxford University Press, champion of the eponymous comma, had changed sides – a typical reaction was: 'Are you people insane? The Oxford comma is what separates us from the animals' – but, as ends of the world go, the truth was distinctly un-apocalyptic. It turned out that a writing guide for press releases and internal communication had advised: 'As a general rule, do not use the serial/Oxford comma: so write "a, b and c" not "a, b, and c".' It added, however, that such a comma might help clarify a sentence or resolve ambiguity, especially where an item in the list was already joined by 'and'. So: he ate ham, eggs and toast; but he ate cereal, kippers, sausages, toast and marmalade, and a muffin.

Sometimes an Oxford comma is essential to avoid ambiguity: 'I dedicate this book to my parents, Martin Amis, and JK Rowling.' (Try it without the comma after 'Amis'.) But often it is neither use nor ornament: *The Times*, in an article about the late actor Peter Ustinov, is said to have referred to his 'encounters with Nelson Mandela, a demigod and a dildo collector'. Inserting an Oxford comma after 'demigod', it is true, would make clear that Mandela does not collect dildos, but only at the risk of labelling him a demigod. In

@guardianstyle They bought a hat for the first bloke to do it (3 wickets in 3 balls in cricket).

such cases, it's easier to forget about the Oxford comma altogether and recast the sentence: 'encounters with a demigod, a dildo collector and Nelson Mandela' would fix the problem.

Putting an Oxford comma in where it doesn't belong can create confusion: in 'two meals, two desserts, and a bottle of wine for £20', the Oxford comma suggests that the wine alone, rather than the whole meal, cost £20.

To sum up, it's as unwise to say always use an Oxford comma as it is to say never use one. The best rule is: use common sense.

Negative, Captain

I won't not use no double negatives.
BART SIMPSON

When Mick Jagger started singing 'I can't get no satisfaction', it was not uncommon to hear the older generation witter on like this: 'He says he *can't* get *no* satisfaction, which logically means he *can* get *some* satisfaction.' Fifty years later Sir Mick is still singing and has sensibly resisted the temptation to change the lyric to 'I can't get any satisfaction'. (Incidentally, checking the lyric of this song online, I came across one website that rendered 'I can't get no girl reaction' as 'I can't get no girly action'. What you might call useless information.)

A double negative may make a positive when you multiply, say, minus three by minus two. However, people who claim the same is true of English are wrong twice over: firstly because language doesn't work in such a logical way – there

@**Arsalan2u** Plural for rickshaw will be rickshaws or rickshaw's?

is nothing logical, for instance, about the fact that 'let's see if we can't get this show on the road' means 'let's see if we can get this show on the road' – and secondly because a double negative does something quite different. As Randolph Quirk pointed out: 'If a boy says, "I haven't done no homework," the teacher is yet to be born who will reply, "Oh good, I'm glad you've done it." The two negatives here do not make a positive: they make a quite emphatic negative.' This is not to say that your teacher will necessarily be impressed by such a construction.

Literature and music abound with multiple negatives. Chaucer used a triple – *He nevere yet no vileynye ne sayde* ('he never said no vileness') – and the second line of Ian Dury's 'Clever Trevor' contains a delicious quadruple:

> *Just 'cos I ain't never 'ad, no, nothing worth having,*
>   *never ever, never ever*
> *You ain't got no call not to think I wouldn't fall into*
>   *thinking that I ain't too clever.*

Not, no, never Standard English, it's true, but no native English speaker is likely to misunderstand, any more than when Jane Austen produced the eloquent double negative 'there was none too poor or remote not to feel an interest'.

Double negatives occur as standard in other languages. For example the French for 'it's nothing' is *ce n'est rien*, literally 'it is not nothing', and no one goes: 'Ah, so it IS something!'

The double negative also appears in English expressions such as 'I can't not go to the wedding now – I've agreed to make a speech'. Similarly, the phrase 'not unattractive'

@guardianstyle Rick Shaw's only if Rick Shaw owns the rickshaws.

is subtly different to 'attractive', but should be used very sparingly – the former prime minister John Major was mercilessly lampooned in *Private Eye* for allegedly overdoing such 'not un-' phrases. In general, it's not a good idea to use too many nots and noes in a sentence, as they can be confusing, can they not?

Between My Souvenirs

And lusty lads roam here and there
So merrily,
And ever among so merrily.

WILLIAM SHAKESPEARE, *HENRY IV PART 2*

I was taught that *between* applies only to two things, and *among* should be used for more than two – a rare example of Mrs Birtles getting it wrong. *Between* is appropriate when the relationship is reciprocal, however many parties are involved: an agreement between the countries of the EU, for example. *Among* belongs to collective relationships, as in votes equally shared among political parties. When fighting broke out at Wembley during the 2012/13 FA Cup semi-final, the punches appear to have been equally shared among the Millwall fans, so it sounded a bit odd when the *Observer* reported clashes 'between Millwall fans'. So the 1927 Paul Whiteman song 'Among My Souvenirs' got it right.

By the way, 'amongst', like 'amidst' and 'whilst', looks very old-fashioned. They are best avoided unless you work for a greeting card company.

@hanmireddy 'C of E looses grip on worshippers.' Is the sentence correct?

While I am on the subject, a little rule that is worth following: it's 'between you and me', not 'between you and I'. It's probably unfair, though quite good fun, to blame the Queen; people have heard 'my husband and I' so much that they perhaps assume 'and I' is always right because it sounds polite. It is correct when it's part of the subject ('my husband *and I* would love to see you at the palace'), but not when it's part of the object ('the Queen offered my husband *and me* cucumber sandwiches'). Between you and me, *between* is a preposition and therefore, as we have just seen, takes an object. And yes, I know that Shakespeare wrote 'All debts are cleared between you and I' in *The Merchant of Venice*. Perhaps Elizabeth I used to say 'the Earl of Essex and I'.

Bored of Tunbridge Wells

> *Society is now one polished horde,*
> *Formed of two mighty tribes, the Bores and Bored.*
> BYRON, *DON JUAN*

Traditionalists say it should be bored *by* or bored *with*, but not bored *of* – a rule cheerfully ignored, I would say, by anyone under about 40. And good luck to them. Oddly, the same thing has not happened with *fed up with* – you rarely hear *fed up by* or *fed up of*; conversely, people say *tired of*, but not *tired with* or *tired by*. Which just goes to show how arbitrary the rules of grammar can be.

I was taught that *bored of* is wrong so it does grate slightly, but there seems no real justification for this. I have,

@guardianstyle It's horribly wrong.

however, managed to come up with a little distinction worth preserving: compare 'bored with Tunbridge Wells' (a person who finds Tunbridge Wells boring) and 'bored of Tunbridge Wells' (a bored person who happens to live there, perhaps a neighbour of 'disgusted of Tunbridge Wells').

Don't Fear the Gerund

> *Here is the glass for pedagogues ... gerund-grinders and bear-leaders to view themselves in.*
>
> LAURENCE STERNE, *THE LIFE AND OPINIONS OF TRISTAM SHANDY, GENTLEMAN*

Geoffrey Willans and Ronald Searle's guide to life at St Custard's school, *How to be Topp*, features a cartoon in which a gerund attacks some peaceful pronouns, but it is nothing to be afraid of. A gerund is a verb ending in *-ing* that acts as a noun: *I like swimming, smoking is bad for you*, and so on. If people remember the term at all, it is probably because they were taught some Latin.

The scary bit is when someone tells you about the rule saying that, as with other nouns, you must use a possessive pronoun – 'she objected to *my* swimming'. Most normal people say 'she objected to me swimming' so I wouldn't worry about this one too much. You rarely see the possessive form in newspapers, for example. Announcing 'I trust too much in my *team's* being able to string a few wins together' sounds awkward and unnatural.

Kingsley Amis says in *The King's English* that the gerund is 'on the way out' and adds wisely: 'Whatever the merits of any rule ... it serves no purpose if nobody obeys it.'

@michaelabbott 'Army'. Singular? Plural? Or either?

And Another Thing …

> *The storm had now definitely abated, and what thunder*
> *there was now grumbled over more distant hills, like a*
> *man saying 'And another thing …' 20 minutes after he'd*
> *lost the argument.*

DOUGLAS ADAMS, *SO LONG, AND THANKS FOR ALL THE FISH*

Conjunctions, as the name suggests, join things together. This prompted generations of English teachers to drill into their pupils, including me, that to start a sentence with *and*, *but*, *because* or *however* was wrong. But this is another shibboleth. And I am sure William Blake ('And Did Those Feet in Ancient Times?') would back me up on this one. Because if the Beatles can start a sentence with the word 'Because', so can you. As no less an authority that Robert Burchfield pointed out in his revised third edition of *The New Fowler's Modern English Usage* (1996): 'The widespread public belief that *but* should not be used at the beginning of a sentence seems to be unshakeable. Yet it has no foundation.'

Tabloid newspapers overdo it: if every sentence starts 'And … ' or 'But … ' the staccato effect becomes monotonous and the conjunctions aren't, in fact, joining anything much at all.

However at the start of a sentence adds emphasis. However, if you do it, be sure to include a comma to give a little pause and avoid confusion with 'However you do it … '

None Sense

> *None are more ignorant of them than those learned*
> *Pedants, whose Lives have been entirely consumed in*
> *Colleges, and among Books.*
>
> HENRY FIELDING, *TOM JONES*

A sure sign of a pedant is that, under the mistaken impression that *none* is an abbreviation of *not one*, the stickler will insist on saying things like 'none of them has turned up'. Why, when I set out on the road to grammatical perfection I might even have argued this myself. But the rule that *none* always takes a singular verb is, alas, another myth.

Plural is not only acceptable, but also often sounds more natural: 'None of the current squad are good enough to play in the Championship.'

I think 'none of the candidates are worth voting for' is better than 'is worth voting for', but if you really prefer the singular you could always use *not one* instead of *none*: 'Not one of the candidates is worth voting for.'

Same Difference

> *How different things appear in Washington than in*
> *London.*
>
> JOHN MAYNARD KEYNES

Different *from* was traditionally taught as correct, but different *to* is widely accepted nowadays. We say differ *from*

@SimonCoopey Are we still leaving two spaces after full-stops, or have we given that up now?

and distinct *from*, not *to*, but it's similar *to* and opposed *to*, so why not different *to*? However, note the difference between:

- *She looked very different from those who came before* (she did not look like them).
- *She looked very different to those who came before* (they thought she looked very different).

Different *than*, standard in American English, is frowned on in Britain. But even here, as the lexicographer Robert Allen points out, there are occasions when 'than' sounds most natural, as in 'a false sense of security which makes drivers behave quite differently on motorways than on ordinary roads' (to avoid *than*, you would have to say 'from the way they behave on ordinary roads'). David Crystal gives the example of 'that's a very different argument than was used by Jim', which sounds no less natural than 'that's a very different argument from the one that was used by Jim'.

Try and Try Again

> *I can't promise I'll try, but I'll try to try.*
> BART SIMPSON

Try to has traditionally been regarded as more 'correct' and *try and* as a colloquialism or worse. The former is certainly more formal, and far more common in writing, but it's the other way round when it comes to speech. One study, based on a 25-million-word database, found that nearly three-quarters of all occurrences of these two phrases in spoken British English were *try and* rather than *try to*, but this was reversed in writing: just over three-quarters of all instances were *try to*. Those who regard *try and* as an 'Americanism' will be disappointed to learn that *try and* is about three times more common in the UK than in the US.

I change *try and* to *try to* when I come across it in *Guardian* stories but it's hard to establish the basis for this as a rule, rather than just a tradition. And if tradition is that important, it's worth noting that *try and* is the older expression (dating from 1686, according to the OED). Sometimes there is a good case for *try and* – for example, if you want to avoid repeating the word *to* in an example such as 'we're really going to try and win this one'.

Perhaps Yoda had the answer when he was teaching Luke the Force in *The Empire Strikes Back*: 'Try not. Do. Or do not. There is no try.'

CHAPTER 3

Whom Do You Love?

A dozen things people should worry about
(but not too much)

> *And therefore never send to know for whom the*
> *bell tolls; it tolls for thee.*
>
> JOHN DONNE, *MEDITATION XVII*

> *Now come on take a walk with me Arlene*
> *And tell me who do you love?*
>
> BO DIDDLEY, 'WHO DO YOU LOVE?'

When I go to the football, I tend to drink too much beer, eat too many pies, swear a lot, hug complete strangers, and spend much of the afternoon singing an inspiring, deeply moving anthem called 'The Greasy Chip Butty Song'. In the office, I avoid this. My employers have never issued me with a list of rules saying I can't behave in the office the way I do at football – they don't need to, because I am observing an established convention.

Or take dating. Most men are aware that being kind and sensitive and taking an interest in what a woman has to say is more appropriate behaviour than, say, telling her how many pints and pies you had at the football that afternoon. (Acting on this knowledge is another matter.) There are conventions governing most human activity – from playing darts to worshipping in church, from eating spaghetti to texting – that make things work better. Don't attempt all those things at the same time, for example. The crucial thing about such rules is that there are different ones for different occasions; most people wouldn't go to their great-aunt's funeral dressed for clubbing.

Language is similar. Different conventions apply to different types of discourse. These are known as registers. Each of the situations in which we use it – texting your mates, asking the boss for a pay rise, composing a small ad, chatting online, making a speech at a wedding, drafting a will, writing up an experiment, praying, rapping, tweeting, and numerous others – has its own conventions that would be inappropriate in other contexts. You don't expect a politician being interviewed by Kirsty Wark about the economy to suddenly start paraphrasing Ludacris by saying he's got his mind on his money and money on his mind, and adding, 'You'se a hell of a distraction when you shake your behind.' Although it might make *Newsnight* more entertaining.

All this renders the concept of what is or isn't 'correct' more than a simple matter of right and wrong. What is correct on Facebook might not be in an essay; no single written English is right every time. It's generally harder to decide what to do on formal occasions. Dressing for the beach is easy: everyone knows that to turn up in collar and tie, woolly pullover and tweed sports jacket (my grandfather's favoured seaside attire) is no longer appropriate. In a similar way, knowing how to update your status on Facebook is instinctive for anyone who can read and write to a basic level. For more formal communication, however, the conventions are

@FredYeast Is 'or not' in 'whether or not' always redundant?

harder to grasp and this is why so many people fret about the 'rules' of grammar.

Here is an extract from Michael Silverstein's review for the *London Review of Books* of a biography of the 19th-century linguist Ferdinand de Saussure, comparing his ideas to those of a contemporary, Charles Sanders Peirce:

> *Thus Peirce differentiates between the fact of linguistic regularities-as-signs – Saussure's* langue *– and the discursive activity of realising them on any given occasion – Saussure's* parole. *And in his description of the special character of symbols, Peirce differentiates between the 'arbitrariness' or community-relative conventionality of the relation between an abstract linguistic signifier (Saussure's* signifiant*) and a correlative abstract conceptual category (Saussure's* signifié*).*

One assumes that Silverstein was writing for a presumed intellectual – or at least highly educated – audience, and that the editor believed that they, unlike me, would be able to make sense of it.

Here is another review, in its entirety, from Rob Reiner's 1983 film *This Is Spinal Tap*, of an album called *Shark Sandwich*:

> *Shit sandwich.*

I can make sense of this one. Admittedly it is fictional, although it's entirely credible that a rock magazine in the 1970s would have carried it (a real review of an LP that

Rolling Stone magazine didn't like made no mention of the music, but devoted the entire piece to detailed instructions on how to melt the vinyl to make an ashtray).

The point is that structure and vocabulary will differ profoundly depending on not only the writer's own style, but also the audience. This is colloquial: 'I said a hip hop the hippie the hippie to the hip hip hop, you don't stop the rock it to the bang bang boogie, say up jumped the boogie to the rhythm of the boogie, the beat.' This is formal: 'Would you care to dance?'

The conventions described in this chapter are ones I think help make formal writing clearer, and worth knowing about even if you don't intend to follow them. 'Why this is worth knowing' in each case could be summarised as 'so you won't look daft'. As Robert Graves said: 'Every English poet should master the rules of grammar before he attempts to bend or break them.'

To Who It May Concern

> *'If it doesn't matter who anybody marries, then it*
> *doesn't matter who I marry and it doesn't matter who*
> *you marry.'*
> *'Whom, not who.'*
> *'Oh, speak English: you're not on the telephone now.'*
> GEORGE BERNARD SHAW, *THE VILLAGE WOOING* (1934)

In Boston, Massachusetts, one of the most GC (grammatically correct) places on Earth, even the owls are said to emit

---

@kickyfeats Cross-country or cross country? To hyphenate, or not to hyphenate?

the cry 'to-whit, to-whom'. Elsewhere, the use of *whom* is dying out, especially in spoken English. Technically, it is the objective form of *who*, and we have already seen that prepositions take an object; thus, if you were talking to someone and she hung up, dismayed by your slovenly use of language, the formal convention is that you would write 'the woman *to whom* I was talking hung up'. It sounds affected and stiff. An article by Megan Garber in *The Atlantic* magazine, which quoted my advice that using *whom* can make you sound like a pompous twerp, suggested that the word might die out altogether in the US within 50 years. The writer William Safire was such a stickler that the joke goes that he insisted on ordering 'two Whoppers Junior' (rather than Whopper Juniors) in Burger King, yet even he advised: 'Whenever *whom* is required, recast the sentence.'

When it comes to writing, people seem to rely on guesswork when deciding between the two words; even a stopped clock is right half the time. Unfortunately, they often guess wrong. Although people worry about using *who* when they should be using *whom*, using *whom* when it should be *who* is much more common, as in this example from the front page of the *Observer*: 'Herbert, while praising the "decent majority" of officers whom [sic] he says do "brilliant" work, suggests that for too long the police have been shielded from criticism by a lack of accountability and an unhealthily cosy relationship with sections of the press.'

Even distinguished writers such as Sir Simon Jenkins, a former editor of *The Times*, sometimes get it wrong: 'Responsibility for our behaviour apparently no longer rests on us as individuals but on anyone whom [sic] a lawyer

---

@guardianstyle Hyphenate, unless you mean, say, Greece.

can claim was "responsible" for our contact with others.' Former *Times* employees yet more distinguished than Sir Simon, such as Graham Greene in *The Quiet American*, have also been guilty: 'There was a big man whom [sic] I think was an *hôtelier* from Phnom Penh and a French girl I'd never seen before.'

If you want to avoid this error, there's a simple test: give the clause beginning *who* or *whom* a mental rejig, replacing it with the third person pronoun: if you get a subject ('he', 'she', 'it' or 'they'), then *who* is correct; if you get an object ('him', 'her' or 'them'), *whom* is right. In the Greene example it would be 'I think he was an *hôtelier*', not 'I think him was an *hôtelier*' – *who*, not *whom*, would therefore have been correct.

So who was right: Donne or Diddley? The answer is both of them. It goes back to the point about formal and informal registers. Bo's got a cobra snake for a necktie! He lives in a house made of rattlesnake hide! Not the kind of guy, I suggest, who would say something wussy like 'Whom do you love?' (It's the same with Ghostbusters, whose slogan, you may recall, was not 'Whom you gonna call?')

The tone of language we use these days is increasingly conversational, which makes *whom* increasingly optional. This was not the case in John Donne's day. His 'for whom the bell tolls' is the climax of a stunning passage that also includes 'no man is an island' and 'any man's death diminishes me, because I am involved in mankind'. The elegant formality of the prose has an eloquence and resonance that 'for who the bell tolls' lacks. Good title for a book, though.

@RuthWriter Hi there! Goody bag or goodie bag?

Why this is worth knowing

There are occasions when *whom* is still desirable. 'A nation's weeping turned to tears of joy with the news that Louie … for who media commentators had to commission new words for camp … is to star in his own 10-part series' (*Guardian Weekend* magazine). That 'for who' sticks out like a cucumber stuffed down a Chippendale's thong. The main reason you need to know the difference, however, is so you don't make the mistake of using *whom* when it should be *who*. This is called hyper-correction: trying too hard.

That's the Way to Do It

The traditional definition, much loved by newspaper style guides (including mine), is that *that* defines and *which* informs (gives extra information), as in:

- 'This is the house that Jack built; but this house, which John built, is falling down.'
- 'The *Guardian*, which I read every day, is the paper that I admire above all others.'
- 'I am very proud of the sunflowers that I grew from seed' (some of them); 'I am very proud of the sunflowers, which I grew from seed' (all of them).

Note that in such examples the sentence remains grammatical without 'that' ('this is the house Jack built'; 'The *Guardian* is the paper I admire above all others'; 'I am very proud of the sunflowers I grew'), but not without 'which'.

I need to say a word or two about relative clauses here. (Believe me, if I didn't have to, I wouldn't.) Don't be alarmed by the terms, which even by the standards of grammar are extremely unhelpful, but *restrictive* relative clauses (also known as *defining*, best thought of as giving essential information by narrowing it down) are not enclosed by commas, whereas *non-restrictive* relative clauses (*non-defining*, giving non-essential information) are.

The last three words of 'he showed me the vase that was broken' constitute a restrictive relative clause, giving information that is essential to the sentence – it was not just any old vase: the whole point is that it was the broken one. In 'he showed me the vase, which was broken', the last three words constitute a non-restrictive clause. Any normal person would also regard this as defining information, since it tells you something important about the vase, which is why the grammatical terms are so useless. However, think of it as extra information that could be left out without affecting the structure and sense of the sentence. The fact that the vase is broken may not be especially relevant.

In the examples at the start of the section, 'which John built', 'which I read every day' and 'which I grew from seed' are all non-restrictive. They give extra information, they are preceded by a comma, and they use 'which' rather than 'that'. In fact, if you try them with 'that' they sound odd ('the *Guardian*, that I read every day'). It's not the same the other way round: although *that* is more common in restrictive clauses, you can use *which*: 'he showed me the vase which was broken'.

@KerryMP Burglarised rather than burgled. Wrong, isn't it?

There used to be a view that *which* was somehow more correct; I was once told sternly by a colleague: 'Our style is *which*'! As you can see, it's more complicated than that, but to simplify things, here's my easy-to-remember formula:

- Restrictive clauses: *that* (desirable) + no comma (essential).
- Non-restrictive clauses: *which* + comma (both essential).

So a recent BBC radio interviewer who asked the question 'Should advertising, which targets children, be banned?' was suggesting that all advertising targets children. She meant 'Should advertising that targets children be banned?'

Why this is worth knowing

It removes ambiguity. The back cover of the Penguin edition of Bill Bryson's *Mother Tongue* contains the following recommendation from the *Sunday Express*: 'A joyful celebration of our wonderful language, which is packed with curiosities and enlightenment on every page.'

The syntax suggests that our wonderful language, rather than the book, is packed with curiosities and enlightenment on every page. It should have been: 'A joyful celebration of our wonderful language that is packed with curiosities and enlightenment on every page.'

This simple fix would have removed any possible ambiguity.

@guardianstyle The wrongest thing we've heard today. But it's still early.

The Dangling Conversation

Though long-legged and possessing a lovely smile, gentleman journalists aren't looking up her skirt and wouldn't even if she weren't gay.

GUARDIAN

Of several strange things about this sentence, which somehow found its way into the *Guardian* when everyone was asleep, not the least strange is the image conjured up of smiling, long-legged gentleman journalists.

A rudimentary grasp of syntax, as well as a visit to the local ENT department's tin ear specialist, might have helped. 'Gentleman journalists aren't looking up her skirt, though she is long-legged and possessing a lovely smile … ' is presumably the meaning intended by the writer. But an entire subordinate clause, 'though long-legged and possessing a lovely smile', has been left dangling at the start of the sentence, like a naked man trying to climb a barbed-wire fence, miles away from the *her* and even further from the *she* that it relates to.

'Having died, they buried him' is a simple example of a dangling or hanging participle because the participle *having* is left suspended too far from the pronoun it refers to, *him*, and instead clings to the adjacent pronoun *they*. The meaning is clear enough but it sounds silly, if not as silly as this: 'This argument, says a middle-aged lady in a business suit called Marion … ' (What were her other outfits called?)

Such sloppy syntax is not always funny. Had it not been promptly corrected, this one could have led to legal action, suggesting as it did (quite wrongly) that a Labour politician had links to a far-right party: 'But in Rotherham, Vines is standing in the Rawmarsh ward in a byelection triggered by the resignation of Labour's Shaun Wright, who became South Yorkshire's police and crime commissioner last year despite his BNP connections.' What was meant was: 'But in Rotherham, Vines, despite his BNP connections, is standing in the Rawmarsh ward in a byelection ... '

Why this is worth knowing

Dangling modifiers and mangled syntax often sound comical – 'Due out in January as a white paper, Ms Kelly may be unable to overcome Mr Blair's apparent determination to stick with A-levels' – which is not necessarily what you are aiming for in a national newspaper's leading article, where this example comes from. So it's best to stop hanging about and reword the sentence. Reading aloud can help to highlight such problems.

Nothing Compares 2U

Shall I compare thee to a summer's day?
WILLIAM SHAKESPEARE, 'SONNET 18'

Prince was right; so was Shakespeare. Compare *to* means 'liken to'; compare *with* means 'make a comparison'. So I

@guardianstyle Thanks, Mum. But I asked you not to tweet me at work.

might compare Lionel Messi *with* Diego Maradona to assess their relative merits, then conclude that Messi can be compared *to* Maradona – he is a similarly great player.

A report that said 'watchers compared the schoolboy with Denis Compton as he smashed the Yorkshire attack around Lord's' invites us to imagine the watchers, perhaps viewing archive footage of the late Compton, attempting to assess the similarities and differences between the two batsmen. What they actually did was liken the schoolboy to Compton. They said he was just like Compton. They *compared* him *to* Compton!

Why this is worth knowing

'The book has been compared to *All Quiet on the Western Front*, *A Farewell to Arms*, *The Red Badge of Courage*, *The Naked and the Dead*, *The Things They Carried*: practically every classic war novel in the American canon.'

Another piece from the *London Review of Books*, this time a review by Theo Tait of *The Yellow Birds* by Kevin Powers, tells us much more than if it had merely said the new book had been compared *with* the classic war novels – the choice of 'compared to' implies that it is of similar quality.

The two phrases have usefully distinct meanings and, although 'compare to' can be replaced by 'liken to', it's clumsier to replace 'compare with' with another phrase.

@CheShA Do I have two mouses attached to my PC, or do I have two mice?

Less Is Not More

The scarier the world becomes, the more important it is to focus on the correct use of 'less' and 'fewer'.

WRITER IAN MARTIN IN THE *GUARDIAN*, REFLECTING ON THE THINGS HE HAD LEARNED BY THE TIME HE WAS 60

Traditionally, fewer (not as many) is used with numbers and less (not as much) with quantity: fewer coins, but less money. This seems a perfectly satisfactory arrangement. But just because you see a number, it doesn't automatically apply: you would be less than 10 miles, or less than 10 minutes, from home, rather than fewer, because you think of distance or time as a whole rather than a collection of individually numbered miles or minutes. The same applies to sums of money: 'I earn less than £100,000.' Unless this book sells a hell of a lot of copies.

The success of the Plain English Campaign's battle a few years ago to persuade Tesco to change its signs from '10 items or less' to 'up to 10 items' gives me hope that one day the company may learn how to use apostrophes – although it does not inspire confidence that a Tesco spokesman heralded the change by saying 'I still don't think we know if "less" or "fewer" is correct'. Perhaps he was confused by the 19th-century Chartists' slogan: 'More pigs and less parsons'.

If there's one thing we can all agree on, it's that when there is only one thing, then it's less, not fewer, as in Burt Bacharach and Hal David's song 'One Less Bell to Answer', perfect grammatically as in every other way.

@guardianstyle Not sure – could you email a pic?

Why this is worth knowing

People will understand you if you say things like 'there were less than 200 of us' but it may strike a jarring note, so don't say you haven't been warned. Observing this distinction also enables you to differentiate between 'Do you have less able children in your class?' (children who are less able) and 'Do you have fewer able children in your class?' (not so many able ones).

Self-Abuse

Reflexive pronouns end in 'self'.
This messy elf just helped himself.
Reflexive pronouns are intensive
when they emphasise or stress.
He himself made this mess ...
The elf seems more offensive
with the use of the intensive.

RUTH HELLER, *MINE, ALL MINE: A BOOK ABOUT PRONOUNS*

Grammatical case has largely disappeared from English. Only those obliged to study Latin – and forced to learn by rote such cases as the vocative ('O table!') and ablative ('by, with or from a table') – will appreciate what a civilised development this is. Case has survived in English pronouns, as we saw with *whom* and 'between you and I'. In the first person singular, *I* is the subjective case and *me* objective. So are people

@SilverTyne Pavements or roads during wintry weather: slippy or [my preference] slippery?

who say things like 'the crew and *myself* [instead of *I*] wish you a pleasant flight' or 'she chose John and *myself* [instead of *me*]' being especially polite or especially wrong? Before answering that, let's take a quick look at reflexive pronouns, also known as 'self-forms'. The main ones are *myself*, *yourself*, *himself*, *herself*, *itself*, *oneself*, *ourselves*, *yourselves*, *themselves*, plus a few variations such as the dialect *thi'sen*, the biblical 'heal *thyself*' and the 'royal we' *ourself*.

We only have to worry about two main types: emphatic and reflexive. Emphatic use puts the focus on a particular participant in a statement: 'I *myself* want no part of it.' Reflexive use 'reflects' a relationship between one element and another in a statement: 'She gave *herself* a treat for Christmas.' Reflexive pronouns are surprisingly versatile and can appear in many contexts: 'He allowed *himself* a drink', 'I am not *myself* today', 'Jane pays for *herself*', 'I pride *myself* on my grammar', 'we only have *ourselves* to blame'. In a literary context, use of a self-form subtly allows a shift in perspective from narrator to character: 'He repeated their names silently – Adam, himself, Shiva, Vivien & – Zosie' (Barbara Vine, *Fatal Inversion*). Other variations include Irish English ('is herself in?') and the grim 'Himself' as used by newspaper columnists to refer to someone they would alternatively describe as 'Him indoors' or 'The other half'.

So what about 'the crew and myself'? The use of *myself* in place of *I* or *me* has been described as 'genteel' (Randolph Quirk) and 'timorous' (Bill Bryson). But when I researched the subject in newspaper archives, it was clear that it had become much more common in recent years, since around the time Will Young was telling *Pop Idol* viewers: 'Myself and

Gareth thank you all so much for everything you've done.' There are two likely explanations. One is that people consider *myself* more polite than *I* or *me*; the other is that they are not always sure which case to use, so opt for the case-neutral *myself*. Or it may be, of course, a bit of both.

No one would use *myself* as a subject rather than *I* in constructions such as 'myself had a smoke', although Saul Bellow did something similar: 'Myself is thus & so, and will continue thus & so.' As did Emily Dickinson: 'But since Myself – assault ME … ' Conjoined with another noun, as in 'Laura and myself had a smoke', it seems less objectionable, though I suspect most people would still prefer 'Laura and I'. As an object, 'he asked Laura and myself' does sound twee compared with 'Laura and me'. My rule is that if you are confident about *I* as a subject and *me* as an object, you can save *myself* for other, far more subtle and interesting uses: 'I found myself', 'I was beside myself', 'I'm all by myself', 'I'm not myself', 'I put myself about', 'I scare myself', and many more.

Why this is worth knowing

Shakespeare wrote: 'No more can I be severed from your side/Than can yourself yourself in twain divide' (*Henry VI Part 1*). It is, frankly, marvellous: a double reflexive. You, however, are not Shakespeare. Stick to the rule above.

@paddydodds How does one become a style guide? I'd like to be a style guide.

Ain't Too Proud to Beg the Question

I analysed all 30-plus mentions of the phrase 'begging the question' in the *Guardian* in a single year. Every one used it to mean 'raises the question', as in this example: 'Nick Clegg's ever growing collection of ties rather begs the question: does he have a discount card for Tie Rack?' So much for the *Guardian* style guide, which states: 'This phrase is almost invariably misused: it means assuming a proposition that, in reality, involves the conclusion. An example would be to say that parallel lines will never meet, because they are parallel.' The concept can be traced back to Aristotle in the fourth century BC. HW Fowler, who used the Latin term *petitio principii* ('assumption of the basis'), defined it as 'the fallacy of founding a conclusion on a basis that as much needs to be proved as the conclusion itself', giving as an example 'foxhunting is not cruel, since the fox enjoys the fun'.

Oddly, in addition to the traditional definition and 'raises the question', Collins dictionary suggests a third meaning, 'evade the issue', which I haven't seen. I am sure writers originally used 'begs' to mean 'raises' for variety, or to try to sound clever. Now everyone does it, which begs – sorry, raises – the question as to how far we should fight for expressions that no one seems to actually use.

Well, not quite no one. I have managed to find a rather pleasing example of the phrase used in its traditional sense, in a January 2013 Oxford University Press blogpost by Anatoly Liberman on the origin of words:

> *We can only reason backward and keep begging the question. Why do we have separate forms for man and*

woman? ... From the fact that the words are different.
The vicious circle is unmistakable.

Why this is worth knowing

Whatever my head says, my heart tells me that just because people can't be bothered to get something right, even when a perfectly good alternative exists, a term that might be useful – even, in a logical or philosophical context, essential – should not be condemned to death. If it goes, our language is that much more impoverished.

A Singular Problem

The local rock group down the street is tryin' hard to
learn their song.

THE MONKEES, 'PLEASANT VALLEY SUNDAY'

'Agreement' or 'concord'. Yes, more off-putting terms for what is a straightforward enough rule: be consistent. Gerry Goffin and Carole King, the great songwriting team who composed the Monkees' 1967 hit 'Pleasant Valley Sunday', took their eyes off the ball by following the singular verb *is* with the plural pronoun *their*. It jars badly, especially when you see it written down rather than sung. If the subject (*rock group*) is singular, and you correctly use a singular verb (*is*), that's what happens when you suddenly switch to plural (*their*) in the same sentence.

@Esquilax5 I always thought starting a sentence with a conjunction was incorrect – am I mistaken?

But wait, I hear you cry. Who says a rock group are singular? There were, after all, four of 'em, zany young actors and musicians who – older readers will recall – were too busy singing to put anybody down. Quite so. If I had happened to wander into the Brill Building in New York City and caught Goffin's or King's ear at the time, I would have politely suggested '*are tryin'* hard to learn their song' as an answer to the problem. In British English, it's normal to treat bands as plural (even when, as in the case of the The, it's just one bloke).

The fact is that collective nouns can be either singular or plural. So you need to use a singular verb when the noun is thought of as a single unit, but a plural verb or pronoun when it is conceived of as a collection of individuals. Some examples:

- *The committee gave its unanimous approval; the committee were enjoying their tea and biscuits.*
- *The family can trace its history back to the middle ages; the family were sitting down, scratching their heads.*
- *The squad is looking stronger than for several seasons; the squad are all very confident they will win promotion this season.*

The same applies to audience, jury, orchestra, team and other nouns that can be thought of in two ways. Even government, which is normally singular, can be plural in an example such as 'when the government say "we're all in it together" they probably mean the Eton old boys' dining society'.

It might seem odd that I said the rule was 'be consistent' when I am talking about nouns that can be singular or plural. But the point is to be consistent within the sentence:

'when the government say "we're all in it together" it probably means ... ' is wrong because it starts plural ('the government *say*') but then suddenly clambers on to a different horse and turns singular ('*it* probably means'). Once you've made your choice, stick with it.

I am often asked if phrases such as 'one in six' are singular or plural, which shows you just how exciting the life of a grammatical perfectionist can be. I think 'one in six' should be plural because it's a noun phrase signifying not one but a group of people. It's a proportion, just like 17 per cent or one-sixth, both of which take plural verbs, as does 'two out of every 12'. A plural verb also better reflects the fact that 'one in six' means one-sixth on average over the whole group.

Why this is worth knowing
If you consistently get singular and plural mixed up, sooner or later someone will notice and conclude you is sloppy.

Sat Down, You're Rocking the Boat

Robin Dutt has a lovely problem on his hands. Sat in his office in Frankfurt ...
Jonnie Peacock is sat in one of Manchester's grander hotels ...

GUARDIAN

@ollieclark 'Please contact myself or Jim.' Surely: 'please contact me or Jim'?

For some reason, people – including the journalists responsible for these two sorry examples from the same day's *Guardian* – struggle with the verb *sit*, so I shall use that as an example in a quick tour of verb tenses.

The good news is that English has just two tenses: present ('I sit') and past ('I sat'). So there is no need to worry about the pluperfect, future conditional, and all that stuff.

Ha! Nearly had you there.

The bad news is that English has lots of tenses, just like other languages. But we use auxiliary verbs (*be, do, have, will*) to make them. So, for example, you make the present continuous tense like this: 'I am sitting.' It's the first person singular of the verb *be*, plus the present participle of the verb *sit*. And the name, though mildly worrying, turns out to be helpful: it's happening now (present), and it's going on (continuous). Easy peasy. Future tense? 'I will sit' (or, if you want to be a little more emphatic about it, 'I shall sit'). Future continuous? Hmm … 'I will be sitting.' (I will be doing it in the future, and it will go on.)

A few more:

- emphatic present ('I do sit');
- emphatic past ('I did sit');
- past continuous or imperfect ('I was sitting');
- present perfect ('I have sat');
- perfect continuous ('I have been sitting');
- past perfect or pluperfect ('I had been sitting'); and
- future perfect ('I will have sat').

@guardianstyle Tell whoever said the former never to contact ourselves.

So you add the infinitive, *sit*, the present participle, *sitting*, or the past participle, *sat*, to an auxiliary verb to get the right tense. If you substituted any other verb, the principle would be the same: the infinitive (*write*, for example), present participle (*writing*) or past participle (*written*) would be correct in place of *sit*, *sitting* or *sat*. Participles are tricky, one reason why Ernie Wise got so many laughs from the phrase 'the book what I wrote'. Present participles usually end in *-ing* (writing, loving, fighting). But there are various endings, including irregular ones, for past participles (written, loved, fought), and sometimes they are the same as the past tense (as with *sat*). That doesn't explain the fact that using *sat* when it should be *sitting*, as in the two examples at the start of this section, is so common.

Why this is worth knowing

Trust me: the 'Jonnie Peacock is sat' example in particular is a very bad mistake in a formal written register, liable to make anyone who knows the first thing about participles, or has much of a feel for language, stop reading at once to write an angry letter to the editor – or worse, if they know where you live. In both examples, the present participle is required. 'At first I sat at the back but I edged forward until I was sitting near the front' is the kind of thing you want: I may have sat in the past, but now I am sitting.

@amyjanejones 'On the grapevine' or 'through the grapevine'?

'Lie Lady Lie'

A similar problem is the confusion between the verbs *lay* and *lie*, although there is more excuse this time as the present tense of the former is the past tense of the latter. The easy way not to mix them up is to remember that *lay* is a transitive verb (it takes an object); *lie* is intransitive.

If you *lay* a table or an egg, or you *lay* something down, the past tense is *laid*, as is the past participle.

If you *lie* down, the past tense is *lay*. The past participle is *lain*.

You will note that technically – as Bob Dylan was inviting the lady in question to lie down across his big brass bed, rather than reporting that she had done so in the past – he should have sung 'Lie Lady Lie' rather than 'Lay Lady Lay'. If you try singing it like that, however, it sounds Australian, which would not really have worked on an album called *Nashville Skyline*.

It's a different verb altogether, but if you *lie* (tell an untruth), the past tense is *lied*.

Why this is worth knowing
Once you know the difference between the two verbs, this common error is easy to avoid.

@guardianstyle I'm just about to lose my mind if anyone else asks this.

Not Much to Report

> *A senior Tory has warned that David Cameron's*
> *leadership would be at stake if the Conservative party*
> *loses next year's European parliamentary elections,*
> *something most polls, political betting sites and Ukip*
> *have said was likely to happen.*
>
> *GUARDIAN*

This sentence, which appeared in the *Guardian* in May 2013, is a mess because the tenses are mixed up. That 'was likely' in particular sits about as comfortably as riding a bicycle with no saddle, because none of the other verbs are in the past tense. It should have read: 'A senior Tory has warned that David Cameron's leadership will be at stake if the Conservative party loses next year's European parliamentary elections, something most polls, political betting sites and Ukip have said is likely to happen.' The tenses are present perfect, present and future, which sit happily together. If you wanted to use the past tense, you could have said: 'A senior Tory warned that David Cameron's leadership would be at stake if the Conservative party lost next year's European parliamentary elections, something most polls, political betting sites and Ukip said was likely to happen.' The point is that you can't just mix and match and hope for the best.

Reported speech relates to the time perspective of the speaker. So when a comment in the present tense is reported, you use the past tense. Allow me to demonstrate. Here is direct speech: *Lizzie said: 'I love chocolate.'* And here is the same thing in reported speech: *Lizzie said she loved chocolate.*

@faintlyfalling Why 'satanist', but 'Christian'? Why not 'Satanist'?

When a comment in the past tense is reported, you use the past perfect tense.

- Direct speech: *Lizzie said: 'I ate too much chocolate.'*
- Reported speech: *Lizzie said she had eaten too much chocolate.*

Similarly, 'will eat chocolate' in direct speech becomes 'would eat chocolate', and so on.

> ### Why this is worth knowing
> I have not quite given up on this one, but the correct use of reported speech seems to be dying out. This is a shame, as using the right tenses in reported speech make it much clearer when something happened or is going to happen. And once you have established who is speaking, there is no need to keep on attributing, so you can say things like: 'Alex said he would vote Labour. There was no alternative. It was the only truly progressive party.' The use of *was* neatly indicates that you are reporting what Alex said.

I'm Like ... and Simon's Like ...

'Like' may sound like a simple little word but it gets people upset. Simon Heffer, the author of *Strictly English*, thinks that 'why does she talk like that?' is a 'vulgarism' and should be 'why does she talk in that way?' This seems pedantic to the point of obscurity.

Using *like* as a preposition ('ride like the wind') is uncontroversial. Using it as a conjunction, introducing a clause that contains a verb ('ride like you're riding a motorbike', 'he behaved like he was drunk') agitates people who say *like* should only govern nouns and pronouns, not verbs and clauses. The simple way to keep everyone happy is to use *like* when the verb is followed by a noun ('he ran like a girl') and *as if* when the verb is followed by a clause ('he ran as if he had seen a ghost').

Ogden Nash pointed out that it's *As You Like It*, not *Like You Like It*, although Shakespeare in fact did use *like* as a conjunction.

Those who object to young people saying 'I was like … and she was like … ' should remember that they were young once.

Why this is worth knowing

The use of *like* as a conjunction sounds inelegant to many people, so it is best kept for informal contexts. It can also lead to ambiguity. As well as a verb, *finished* can be an adjective meaning 'done for'; to me, 'it looks like he's finished' has this meaning because it sounds more colloquial than 'it looks as if he's finished', which suggests he has completed whatever it was that he started.

Using *like* rather than *such as* in sentences like – I mean such as – 'I prefer weekend breaks in cities like Manchester' is also ambiguous. If the speaker is from Manchester, she probably means she likes to visit places that remind her of home; if not, she is probably including Manchester among similar places she likes to visit, in which case 'I prefer weekend breaks in cities such as Manchester' is clearer.

CHAPTER 4

Pin the Apostrophe on the Word

All you need to know about punctuation
in one handy chapter

> *I must suppose my system of punctuation to be very*
> *bad; but it is mine; and it shall be adhered to with*
> *punctual exactness.*
> ROBERT LOUIS STEVENSON

> *'If you could edit your past, what would you change?'*
> *'I'd get rid of all the commas.'*
> PETER CAREY

Despite claims to the contrary Peter Carey did not get rid of
all the commas in his 2001 Booker prize-winning novel *True
History of the Kelly Gang* (there are 13 on the first page alone)
and attempting to write without them is a pretty bad idea in
general because as you can see you are likely to end up with
very long unwieldy sentences like this one that are difficult
to read and leave your poor readers out of breath well before
they get to the end.

Punctuation is not difficult, although some books
contrive to make it sound complicated. Although most apostrophes are obligatory, with other punctuation you normally

have plenty of choices – between, for example, commas and dashes – and if you really don't like brackets (for example) you don't have to use them. Punctuation isn't there to catch you out, or to allow you to demonstrate that you are cleverer than other people because you know how to use a semicolon; its sole purpose is to provide information and help the reader understand what you are trying to convey.

Picasso described punctuation marks as 'the fig-leaves that hide the private parts of literature', but I rather like them. It would be a bit much to talk about the joys of a well-placed semicolon; using punctuation correctly, however, or correcting someone else's – which I have been doing in one way or another since 1974 – can be very satisfying.

Feeling You're Nuts: Apostrophes

Imagine a boy is admitted to hospital with acute appendicitis. In the next bed, another boy is suffering from severe tonsillitis. In the operating theatre, the surgeon's notes say: 'Remove the boys' tonsils.' The surgeon does as instructed and later that night the first boy develops peritonitis and nearly dies. No wonder, having had his tonsils taken out, along with those of the other boy, rather than his appendix.

Far-fetched? I hope so; I've never worked in a hospital. But you can see how easily a misplaced apostrophe (boys' rather than boy's) might lead to, at the very least, a serious misunderstanding. We have to trust that medical staff know how to use apostrophes, unlike the people who run Tesco, Britain's biggest supermarket: it's in a class of its own when it

---

@sreddyen Do you prefer 'e.g.' and 'i.e.', or 'eg' and 'ie'?

comes to apostrophe abuse. You'd think that someone among its half-a-million or so employees would know better than to put up signs saying 'Kids toys'. It gets worse in the clothing department: a simple 'Kids' seems fair enough – it would need an apostrophe only if it said 'Kids' clothes' – but the signs nearby are a scarcely credible 'Mens' and 'Womens'. They call this the F&F range. I have my own version of what the Fs stand for. The meaning may be clear but the sloppiness demonstrated by this insult to the intelligence of its customers makes you wonder what else, as a business, Tesco gets wrong. Sell-by dates? Prices?

It's easy to smirk at the 'greengrocer's apostrophe' – the shop that uses an apostrophe to indicate a plural ('pea's'), often omitting one when it is actually required ('new seasons asparagus') – but a small trader worried about where the next delivery of purple sprouting broccoli is coming from has got more excuse than a huge multinational business that makes a profit of £1bn a year. I wonder how far I'd get with a job application to Tesco if I wrote something like this: 'Id really like a job at Tescos, I think its a great company, it sell's everything from kids toys to Mens. p.s I also like the BOGOF's.'

Tesco is not alone: the difficulties many people have with apostrophes can be explained by a walk along any high street. You might pass Boots (that's Jesse Boot you can hear spinning in his grave, although he lost his apostrophe many years ago); Waterstones (or, as it was known until 2012, Waterstone's); Sainsbury's (founded by a couple of Sainsburys, and which might therefore be known as Sainsburys', although its official name is J Sainsbury); Marks & Spencer (widely known as Marks & Spencer's); and Tesco (which has also never had an apostrophe – that may explain why it doesn't know how to use them – but, perhaps by allusion with Sainsbury's, is often referred to as Tesco's). Then there's Lloyds TSB, nothing to do with the insurer Lloyd's of London, and numerous similar examples. A Goodfella's pizza has an apostrophe because, presumably, the people who market it like us to think it is made by a 'Goodfella', whereas the classic gangster movie *Goodfellas* was just a plural.

No wonder people are confused: a colleague coined the word apostrofly – 'an insect that lands at random on the printed page, depositing an apostrophe wherever it lands'. There is even an International Apostrophe Day, launched (by me) a few years ago to encourage better use of this humble piece of punctuation.

I confess I used to think 'weer' in the song title 'Mama Weer All Crazee Now' was Slade's idiosyncratic spelling of 'were', in Black Country dialect (which, by the way, I am allowed to make fun of because my family originally came from there): 'My mother weer a bit croizy, loike.' It turns out, more prosaically, to be Slade's idiosyncratic spelling of 'we're' as in 'Mother dear, we are all rather eccentric these days'. If only they had used an apostrophe, the meaning would have been clear.

Apostrophes are quite simple. Some books list as many as eight uses for them but they are just trying to confuse you: there are only three to worry about.

To Indicate Missing Letters

I'd [I would] rather buy my own beer if you won't [will not] put your hand in your pocket.

@lottelydia The Guardian Budget liveblog has a side header saying 'Budget 2013: How does it effect you?'

Many pronouns are routinely abbreviated and need an apostrophe – it's (it is), who's (who is), they're (they are), you're (you are), and so on. The way to avoid confusing them with their apostrophe-less equivalents (its, whose, their or there, and your) is to do a quick check of the meaning. In the sentence 'There are many people who count their blessings even when they're poor', 'they're' is clearly a contraction of 'they are' so needs an apostrophe.

Examples of abbreviated words that are sometimes given apostrophes include 'flu (short for influenza), Hallowe'en (All Hallows Evening) and Jo'burg (Johannesburg). These all look a little old-fashioned and you don't need to bother, although I have kept fo'c'sle (forecastle) in the *Guardian* style guide for nostalgic reasons as it is a survivor from the very first *Style-book of the Manchester Guardian* in 1928.

To Indicate a Possessive

His dad's quirky grammar book was top of Oliver's Christmas list.

But note that the possessive *its*, like other possessive pronouns such as *hers*, *ours*, *yours* and *theirs*, does not have an apostrophe: 'Tesco doesn't know its onions.' To confuse you further, *one's* does ('one knows one's onions'), but you wouldn't use that unless you wanted to sound particularly pompous.

The term 'possessive' is misleading; 'association' or 'relationship' would be more helpful. For example, David might be said to possess 'David's book', but hardly 'David's favourite football team', although David needs an apostrophe in both cases.

@guardianstyle Not any more, it doesn't.

If a word ends in S, an apostrophe and second S are added to make it possessive if that is how it is pronounced: James's book, but waiters' tips. If a plural does not end in S, you add an apostrophe + S: children's games, people's republic, women's rights, etc.

Phrases such as butcher's hook, collector's item, cow's milk, goat's cheese and writer's cramp are best treated as singular. We either don't know or don't care whether one cow, or many, are involved.

To Indicate Time or Quantity

This book represents a year's thought, squeezed into a month's actual work.

Apostrophes are used in phrases such as two days' time and 12 years' jail, where the time period (two days) modifies a noun (time), but not in three weeks old or nine months pregnant, where the time period (three weeks) modifies an adjective (old). You can test this by trying the singular: one day's time, but one month pregnant.

Occasionally people who should know better say apostrophes don't make any difference. George Bernard Shaw, when not campaigning to spell bomb 'bom', called them 'uncouth bacilli'; John Wells, my phonetics professor at UCL and one of the cleverest men I've ever known, called them 'a waste of time'; Peter Buck of REM said: 'We all hate apostrophes. There's never been a good rock album that had an apostrophe in the title.' (Yes, Peter, *Sgt. Pepper's* was such rubbish compared with REM's *Around the Sun*.)

@andypandy212 Sorry if it's been asked before but Dear All or Dear all in a group email?

But consider these four sentences, where the apostrophes enable you to express different concepts with great precision:

- *The guitarist's friend's CD*
  (refers to one guitarist and one friend).
- *The guitarist's friends' CD*
  (one guitarist with more than one friend).
- *The guitarists' friend's CD*
  (more than one guitarist; one friend).
- *The guitarists' friends' CD*
  (more than one guitarist; their friends).

Kingsley Amis had this simple test: 'An accomplished apostrophe-wielder must be able to distinguish instantly between the following:

- *He is staying with Jones.*
- *He is staying at Jones's.*
- *He is staying with the Joneses.*
- *He is staying at the Joneses'.*

There are those who would put an apostrophe in plural abbreviations: CD's. All I can say to that is thank goodness for downloads. In fact, unless you want to be lampooned along with all those poor greengrocers, never use apostrophes in plurals, including abbreviations: the DJ's beats were tight; the other DJs were jealous. A cafe offering 'PIE'S, PASTY'S, SANDWICH'S + CAKES' does not inspire confidence. It's at times like this that I start to sympathise with those linguists who argue that apostrophes are not punctuation at all, just an aspect of spelling.

To sum up: apostrophes are the difference between feeling you're nuts and feeling your nuts; between 'Hell mend them' (an old-fashioned curse) and 'He'll mend them' (a bloke's coming round to fix your tiles).

Apostrophe abuse
Irritation factor: 9/10
Frequency of error: 8/10
Misused by: supermarkets, greengrocers

Typical example:

> *Part Time Chef's/Cook's Required.*
> *Must Have A Good Understanding Of English.*
> (SIGN OUTSIDE A RESTAURANT)

And the worst offender is: Tesco

Let's Eat, Grandma: Commas

> *When the Dutch reflect on their performance in this*
> *World Cup final, they will not find it hard to see why*
> *their aggressive tactics lost them many friends in 2010.*

A comma helps the reader by inserting breathing space into a sentence, literally in an example such as the one above where

---

@ojdwallace All tolled or all told, please?

there's a natural pause after 'final'. Commas make sentences easier to read, by breaking them up into manageable sections, and help to make the meaning clear, as in this sentence. Used, wrongly, as in this sentence they are very irritating. To help develop an instinctive feel for the flow of a sentence, try reading it aloud and insert a comma when you pause (as I just did after the word 'sentence'). If you use commas as parenthesis, to explain something as I am doing here, make sure you add the second comma just as you would add a second bracket.

Commas have lots of other uses. As with apostrophes in my theoretical example, a misplaced comma could even be damaging to your health. Compare:

- 'Do not administer any liquids which are diuretic' (some liquids are permissible) and
- 'Do not administer any liquids, which are diuretic' (all liquids are forbidden).

If you could use 'and' between adjectives in a list, use a comma: a bright red car doesn't need one because you wouldn't say 'a bright and red car'; a tall, dark, handsome man does, because you could say 'tall and dark and handsome'. This example from the *Guardian* shows how a misplaced comma in such a list can actually sabotage the intended meaning: 'Neocon economists often claim a large, black economy turbo-powers growth.' The writer meant a large black economy, not a large and black one, which is what this says.

You can use a comma to introduce a quote, 'He said,' although I prefer a colon: 'He added.'

A comma can also change the general to the specific. Note these two sentences:

- 'The author David Marsh says this is more interesting than many grammar books.'
- 'The author, David Marsh, says this is more interesting than many grammar books.'

In the first example, David Marsh is an author in general; in the second, he is specifically identified as the author of this book. It is interchangeable with 'David Marsh, the author, says … ' whereas in the first example 'David Marsh the author says' sounds a little unnatural, unless it's to differentiate him from all the other David Marshes.

Similarly, the comma after 'the editor-in-chief, Alan Rusbridger, is a man of vision' indicates that there is only one editor-in-chief; 'the subeditor David Marsh is all style and no substance' reveals him to be just one among many. Switching to the indefinite article would make the same point and this time you would use commas: 'A subeditor, David Marsh, has … '

A comma splice, which sounds painful, occurs when a comma is not up to the job of joining two main clauses: 'this was sensible advice, it was almost too easy' would be improved by using a semicolon or a conjunction such as 'but' instead of the comma.

Here's a reminder about the importance of commas in relative clauses, which I explained in chapter 3. To see how to get it wrong, consider this example from the *Guardian*:

> *Part of the report will heavily criticise a so-called power*
> *culture among the Dublin bishops who have been*
> *accused of not taking the allegations seriously.*

As written, the words beginning 'who have been accused' comprise a restrictive relative clause: it says only some Dublin bishops have been accused. The writer in fact meant to say all of the bishops had been accused, so needed to insert a comma after 'bishops' to introduce a non-restrictive relative clause:

> *Part of the report will heavily criticise a so-called power*
> *culture among the Dublin bishops, who have been*
> *accused of not taking the allegations seriously.*

Looking at the sentence now with the relative clause removed – 'Part of the report will heavily criticise a so-called power culture among the Dublin bishops' – you can see this still conveys the desired meaning: that all the Dublin bishops and their so-called power culture have been criticised.

So if you add a relative clause giving additional, non-essential information, you must introduce it with a comma. You wouldn't think such a simple thing could completely change the meaning, but it can and does all the time, which is why understanding how commas work is so important.

Keith Waterhouse advised: 'Commas are not condiments. Do not pepper sentences with them unnecessarily.' Quite so, but a well-placed one is the difference between 'what is this thing called love?' and 'what is this thing called, love?' And between 'let's eat, Grandma!' and ... well, you know the rest.

Upmarket Punctuation Marks: Colons and Semicolons

Colons should be used like this: between two sentences, or parts of sentences, where the first introduces a proposition that is resolved by the second. Or as HW Fowler put it: 'To deliver the goods invoiced in the preceding words.'

Colons are useful when presenting examples: for instance, this one.

They also precede a list. 'He was an expert on the following: the colon, the comma and the full stop.'

And as we have seen, a colon can be used to introduce a quotation: 'He is a stickler for colons.'

It's depressing to see semicolons used where only a colon will serve, as in this example from my own paper: 'Here's a task for the new coalition government; set up a drumming taskforce today, and appoint a Snare Tsar.' Any humorous effect this sentence might have had was outweighed by a strong desire on my part to give the writer a firm but fair rap on the knuckles with a ruler.

Far from being interchangeable with a colon, a semicolon is an elegant compromise between a full stop (too much) and a comma (not enough).

- Here are two independent but related sentences. I have used a full stop after the first one to link them.
- Here are two more independent but related sentences, but this time I have used a comma and the conjunction 'but' to link them.
- Here are two more independent but related sentences; a semicolon is another way to link them.

@mattdykes Eric Pickles' or Eric Pickles's?
the extra 's' looks nasty.

Writers disagree about the value of semicolons. Our old friend George Bernard Shaw, not someone you would ever accuse of understatement, wrote to TE Lawrence: 'You practically do not use semicolons at all. This is a symptom of mental defectiveness, probably induced by camp life.' A shame he rejected the option of using a semicolon instead of a full stop after the first sentence.

Beryl Bainbridge said: 'A semicolon is a partial pause, a different way of pausing, without using a full stop. I use it all the time.' Jeanette Winterson agrees: 'I think it makes an elegant pause', and Will Self says: 'I like them – they are a three-quarter beat to the half and full beats of commas and full stops. Prose has its own musicality, and the more notation the better.' Anne Enright explains: 'The semicolon is useful when you need a sentence to shift or surprise; to be modified or amended; it allows a generosity, lyricism and ambiguity to creep into the sentence structure. It can also be the sign of a self-indulgent writer and should be used with care.'

Kurt Vonnegut, by contrast, called them 'transvestite hermaphrodites, standing for absolutely nothing. All they do is show you've been to college.' The American poet Richard Hugo said: 'Semicolons indicate relationships that only idiots need defined by punctuation. Besides, they are ugly.' A verdict that might have been a little more persuasive had he thought to use a semicolon instead of the full stop.

In France, where a fierce debate about the future of the semicolon (*point-virgule*) has been raging, the satirist François Cavanna regards it as 'a parasite, a timid, fainthearted, insipid thing, denoting merely uncertainty, a lack of audacity, a fuzziness of thought'. But fellow writer Michel Volkovitch says:

@guardianstyle So does Eric Pickles ...

'It puts things in order, it clarifies. But it's precious, too, for adding a little softness, a little lightness; it can stop a sentence from touching the ground, from grinding to a halt; keeps it suspended, awake. It is a most upmarket punctuation mark.'

You can lead a full and happy life without bothering with semicolons. I quite like to use one when I feel that something more than a comma, but less than a full stop, is needed; as here. They are also very handy in lists, particularly when items consist of several words or contain punctuation themselves: 'His holiday reading comprised *Eats, Shoots & Leaves*; *Sheffield United FC: the Official Centenary History*; and *Through the Looking-Glass, and What Alice Found There*.'

The Art of Parenthesis: Brackets and Dashes

According to Mark Forsyth's *The Etymologicon*, the word *brackets* comes from the French *braguette* (codpiece) because of its supposed resemblance to architectural brackets. Captain John Smith, of *Pocahontas* fame, was the first to spell it 'brackets' in his 1627 dictionary *A Sea Grammar*.

Brackets give information in parenthesis, and indeed are called parentheses in the US [where brackets are square, like this]. Keep ones {like this} and <like this> for mathematics or computing. They are used to clarify (or give extra information). I use them a lot. I think they help to add 'that essential quality of the amusing storyteller, the art of parenthesis, the dropping in of the appropriate and unexpected word, the swift and illuminating phrase', as a 1902 newspaper article quoted in the OED put it.

@MatthewRogerson Should it be actress' or actress's?

It is possible to get carried away and overdo it, however, as in the Beastie Boys' '(You Gotta) Fight for Your Right (to Party!)'.

If a sentence is logically and grammatically complete without the information contained within the parentheses (round brackets), the punctuation stays outside the brackets. (A complete sentence that stands alone in parentheses starts with a capital letter and ends with a full stop.) 'Square brackets', the grammarian said, 'are used in direct quotes when an interpolation [a note from the writer or editor, not uttered by the speaker] is added to provide essential information.'

Dashes are used for parenthesis as an alternative to brackets or a pair of commas – like this – but if you start with one, be sure to add a second to save the reader from hunting through the sentence like someone rooting around in a sock drawer.

A single dash can also add a touch of drama – look! Use sparingly, however. Some journalists have a tendency to stick a dash in every time they don't feel like writing a proper sentence – like this.

Beware sentences – such as this one – that dash about all over the place – it makes them look like a poem by Emily Dickinson. *Gwynne's Grammar*, published in 2013 and styling itself as a 'traditional, common-sense' approach to the subject, opens unpromisingly with a description of the author comprising a single sentence, more than 100 words long, containing no fewer than five dashes.

!?

The story, which may even be true, that when Victor Hugo wanted to know how *Les Misérables* was doing he sent a telegram to his publisher saying '?' and received the reply '!' demonstrates that these symbols are economical, albeit potentially ambiguous (would the publisher have used anything different if the work had been a flop?). They are nothing if not versatile: a US garage punk band named ? And The Mysterians had a hit in the 1960s, and there is also a band called !!!

Newspapers are said to employ various synonyms for exclamation marks, such as bang, shriek, dog's cock or screamer. I must say that, after 40 years in the business, I have never heard anyone use any of these terms. What is true is that when a newspaper employs an exclamation mark in a headline, it invariably means: 'Look, we've written something funny!' As F Scott Fitzgerald said, using an exclamation mark 'is like laughing at your own jokes'. Elmore Leonard recommends using 'no more than two or three per 100,000 words'. Terry Pratchett says overusing them is 'a sure sign of someone who wears his underpants on his head'.

Some books list as many as six uses for the exclamation mark, which all turn out to be basically the same: to add emphasis to expressions of emotion such as anger, joy or surprise: 'I have never seen anything like it!' My colleague Simon Hoggart's brilliant Commons sketches use exclamation marks ironically to poke fun at over-excitable politicians: 'Claire Perry of Devizes, a Conservative MP who would make Pollyanna sound like a crabby old fishwife, chirruped

---

@stuhall Do you prefer spelt or spelled?
Or switch between them?

that KPMG had just named Britain as the best country in the world to do business! The very best!'

Exclamation marks are seldom, if ever, obligatory. They can, however, be annoying! And make it look as if your work was written by a 12-year-old!!! So use sparingly.

As for question marks, the clue is in the name: use after a question. OK? But not indirect questions, in case you were wondering whether they needed one.

'Quotation' Marks

At the risk of stating the obvious, quotation marks – also known as inverted commas, speech marks, and (in newspaper offices) quotes – are used when directly quoting someone, as here:

John Ruskin said: 'Say all you have to say in the fewest possible words, or your reader will be sure to skip them; and in the plainest possible words, or he will certainly misunderstand them.'

Whether to use single or double quotation marks is a matter of choice or, in the case of a publication, house style. In Britain, newspapers favour double (with single for quotes within quotes); book publishers tend to the opposite. When a complete sentence is quoted, full stops and commas go inside the quotation marks, as here:

'Anna said: "This book of yours is taking a long time," and I said: "I agree, but it will be worth it in the end." ' Americans call this 'logical punctuation', and would be unhappy about my placing of the comma outside 'punctuation' a few words ago. Just the kind of compromise you'd expect from some Brit panty-waist.

None the less, I maintain that if only part of a sentence is quoted, the quotation marks come outside: 'David said writing the book was "a difficult and time-consuming task".'

Quotation marks can be used to indicate irony, as in: 'My "free lunch" turned out to be the most expensive, not to say indigestible, meal of my life.' These are sometimes known as scare quotes. Making little quotation mark signs in the air is optional. You could dispense with the whole rigmarole by saying 'my so-called free lunch turned out to be … '

The most important thing about quotation marks is 'never' to use them for 'emphasis' or you will end up saying the opposite of what you intend and looking foolish, quite possibly on The 'Blog' of 'Unnecessary' Quotation Marks or another of the websites devoted to the subject. A few examples:

WE SELL 'BOXES'

assorted candy 'no sugar added'

'CHEESE'
BURGERS

SKY
DIVE
from a
'Perfectly good airplane'

'HAT' RACK

@furiousniall Is it TV on the Radio or TV On The Radio?

'We Greatly'
'appreciate you're'
'Business'
'Please Come'
'Back'
'Thank'
'You'
All

Quotation marks like this start off looking funny but after a while seem rather sad. The last in particular has an air of desperation about it. Anyway, I am going to take a break now and go for a 'cup of tea'.

Something Understood: Ellipsis

So anyway, these three ellipses walk into a bar …

Three dots … with a space before and after (you would be amazed how many times I am asked what the 'rule' is about how many spaces) indicate something is missing, typically in a quotation or extract from a document. They can be used (sparingly) to add an air of mystery to the end of a sentence … We also use them in headlines to add suspense … or to fill out a short line: 'So long … and thanks for all the fish.' The term dates from the 17th century, when the poet Abraham Cowley wrote this charming, and still valid, definition: 'An Elleipsis, or leaving something to be understood by the Reader.'

@guardianstyle TV On The Radio (band);
TV on the radio (you've got a cool radio).

The End: The Full Stop

The full stop, full point (as we call it at work) or period (as they call it in the US) goes at the end of a sentence. Some people use full stops in abbreviations and initialisms (e.g. B.B.C.), though this is much less prevalent than used to be the case and I can't see any need. And that's about it. Except to say that hyphens and capital letters are not punctuation marks, despite what you may have read in some books.

See the next chapter.

CHAPTER 5

Too Marvellous for Words

Don't let wobbly spelling distract you from the
wonder of language

> *You're just too marvellous, too marvellous for words*
> *Like 'glorious', 'glamorous' and that old standby*
> *'amorous'…*
> *You're much too much, and just too 'very, very'*
> *To ever be in Webster's Dictionary.*
>
> FRANK SINATRA, 'TOO MARVELLOUS FOR WORDS'

> *A word hasn't got a meaning given to it, as it were, by a*
> *power independent of us, so that there could be a kind of*
> *scientific investigation into what the word really means.*
> *A word has the meaning someone has given to it.*
>
> LUDWIG WITTGENSTEIN

What's the loveliest word in the English language? I will tell
you in a moment. But first, experts agree with Juliet that, in
most cases, a rose by any other name would smell as sweet – if
it were still spelt and pronounced *roose*, for example, as it was
a few hundred years ago. Samuel Johnson said: 'Words are
but the signs of ideas.' English has a few onomatopoeic words
(mimicking the sound they represent) such as *cuckoo*, *splash*,
tick-tock and *KerPlunk*. Lewis Carroll came up with *slithy* and
mimsy, among others, in 'Jabberwocky', and a memorable

sentence in Evelyn Waugh's *Scoop* gave us 'Feather-footed through the *plashy* fen passes the questing vole'. But the relationship between word and meaning can rarely be predicted from the sound. Most people think *demure* is a nicer word than *manure*, say, not because one is intrinsically more pleasing than the other, but because it is impossible to separate a word from the meaning it has been assigned.

Favourite words are subjective. For JRR Tolkien, the phrase 'cellar door' (also said to have been popular with Edgar Allan Poe and Dorothy Parker) was more beautiful than *beautiful* or *sky*. Wilfred J Funk, who for many years wrote the popular *Reader's Digest* column 'It Pays to Increase Your Word Power', produced his own M-heavy list (*marigold, melody, mignonette, murmuring* and *myrrh* all made the cut) in 1932. The protagonist of *The Singing Detective*, Dennis Potter's acclaimed 1986 BBC drama, thought the loveliest word was *elbow* (the band took their name from this episode). A British Council survey in 2004 found that non-native English speakers liked *love, mother, smile, passion* and *tranquillity*.

On the *Guardian*'s Mind Your Language blog in 2012, Harriet Powney put forward her five favourite words: *balalaika, beetroot, cwtch* (Welsh for something between a hug and a cuddle), *kecks* and *rococo*. I pitched in with my own (*butterfly, exquisite, gurgle, music* and *sheer*) and we invited readers to nominate theirs, which they did in their hundreds: *autumnal, bumblebee, crepuscular, kerfuffle* and *mellifluous* all proved popular. On the basis of this completely unscientific survey, plus research online and in the library, including Robert Beard's book *The 100 Most Beautiful Words in English*, I declare the most popular English word to be:

....

@TomWillshaw Ancient Greece or ancient Greece?

SERENDIPITY

The OED entry says: 'Serendip, a former name for Sri Lanka + ITY suffix', defining it thus: 'The faculty of making happy and unexpected discoveries by accident. Also, the fact or an instance of such a discovery.' It goes on to say that the word, coined by Horace Walpole in 1754, was 'formerly rare', but achieved 'wide currency' in the 20th century. *Serendip* comes from the Arabic *Sarandib*, itself adopted from the Sanskrit *Simhahadvipa*, meaning 'dwelling-place-of-lions island'. This romantic etymology only enhances the word's appeal. It has been described as one of the hardest English words to translate, although equivalents in other languages include the French *serendipicité* and Portuguese *serendipicidade*.

Words, Words, Words

> *'What do you read, my lord?'*
> *'Words, words, words.'*
> WILLIAM SHAKESPEARE, *HAMLET*

The *Guardian* publishes about 250,000 words on a typical weekday, many of them spelt correctly. On Friday 21 December 2012, we muscled in at 281,488 words, which at an average speed would take you about 18 hours to read. For comparison, F Scott Fitzgerald's *The Great Gatsby* has a mere 47,094 words (which hasn't prevented Baz Luhrmann making a 142-minute film of it). And people wonder why we make mistakes.

@guardianstyle ancient Greece is fine by the British Museum, and fine by us.

English is a marvellous mashup of words. A few Celtic placenames. A stock of Old English words (*day* and *night*, *black* and *white*, *food* and *drink*, *life* and *death*, *beer*). More than twice as many words adopted from Norman French (*marriage*, *parliament*). Sometimes competing words from both: *motherhood* (Old English) and *maternity* (Norman French). Words of Greek derivation, like *octopus*. Words of Latin derivation, such as *campus* and *ultimatum*. Words from all over the place: Welsh (*corgi*), Irish (*brogues*), Arabic (*algebra*), German (*hamster*), Chinese (*typhoon*), Japanese (*tycoon*), American Indian (*tobacco*), Hawaiian (*ukulele*), and many more.

Wherever they come from, words fall in and out of fashion. Within living memory *gay* has changed meaning completely, while *bad* and *wicked* changed, then changed back. Yesterday's slang is respectable today. In the 1950s and 60s, words that angered people who write to newspapers included *job* (the writer thought it vulgar, and preferred *employment*), *breakdown* ('horrible jargon'), and *layby* ('a combination of verb and preposition of rather obscure meaning') – alternative suggestions from *Daily Telegraph* readers included *siding*, *pull up* and *lie bay*. The Manchester *Guardian* stylebook of 1950 banned such 'slang' phrases as *bank on*, *face up to*, *give away*, *sack* (for 'dismiss'), and many others.

The expression 'a foregone conclusion' once meant an experience previously undergone, rather than making a decision without listening to the arguments. Many words we use today have a different meaning from 20, never mind 50, 100 or 200 years ago. Attempts in the 18th century to 'fix' the

---

@rob_davies Start up or start-up business?

language foundered. *Nice* once meant silly (*silly* meant happy or blessed), then subtle, then pleasant. You could be *sad* with food and drink – it meant full to the brim, and was related to sated, satiated, satisfied and saturated. It then came to mean solid, so a reliable person could be called *sad*; in time, solid, heavy and dull came to mean sad in one of our modern uses. In recent years it subtly acquired an additional meaning, as in 'how sad is that?'

Cicero invented the word *qualitas* because he felt Latin was inadequate to express a Greek philosophical concept. Now that's what I call nerdy. About 1,700 words are first recorded in Shakespeare (which does not necessarily mean he invented them), including *barefaced, fancy-free, laughable* and *submerged*. Milton is credited with *beleaguered, impassive, jubilant, sensuous* and many more, as well as the expressions 'trip the light fantastic' and 'all ears'. Jung, and not as you might think Sting, invented the word *synchronicity* as well as *ambivalent, extrovert* and *introvert*, while Freud came up with the word *psychoanalysis*, which is derived from the Greek for butterfly, *psyche*, who was also the Greek goddess of the soul.

Technology is a continual source of new words. The man who developed the wireless technology Bluetooth in 1996 was reading a historical novel about Harald Bluetooth, a 10th-century king of Denmark, at the time and appropriated his name. Spam, in the sense of unwanted emails, was named after the 1970 Monty Python cafe sketch in which Spam, in the sense of unwanted canned meat, was compulsory in every dish. Sometimes new words catch on, sometimes they don't, but you can always bet that someone, somewhere will object to them. I recall readers complaining

---

@guardianstyle Start up: verb; startup: noun;
star tup: top-performing ram.

about the *Guardian*'s use of the new word *blog* (an abbreviation of another new word, *weblog*) but within a very short time it had become established. In the 1950s, when a single word to express 'capable of undergoing nuclear fission' was being sought, there was a discussion as to whether *fissionable* or *fissible* would be more suitable – leading to a letter in *The Times*: 'Fissionable is fashionable and surely reasonably admissible. Fissible is risible.' In the early 1960s, the AA sought suggestions from the public for a new word to describe drivers: submissions included *autocarist*, *autonaut*, *chassimover*, *motorman*, *wheelist*, and the bizarre acronym *pupamotor* ('person using power-assisted means of travelling on roads'). The idea was dropped. Whoever came up with *laser* ('light amplification by stimulated emission of radiation') in 1960 was more successful.

The writer AP Herbert devised a scoring system for new words, which would be given marks out of 10 on each of four criteria: is it readily understood, is it to be admired, is it sound etymologically, and is it actually required? The pass mark was 50 per cent and *television*, for example, just scraped through (scoring respectively 10, 0, 0 and 10). One of my favourite recent words, which I fear would probably fail the Herbert test, is *bouncebackability*, a neat alternative to 'the ability to bounce back', attributed to the former football manager Iain Dowie. Thanks to friends of mine on Twitter with a flair for language and too much time on their hands, it has been translated into French (*la rebondissabilité*) and German (*die Rücksprungsfähigkeit*).

@notvoodoo Hey, when did you guys stop capitalising the word Internet?

I Put a Spell on You

My spelling is Wobbly. It's good spelling but it Wobbles,
and the letters get in the wrong places.

WINNIE-THE-POOH

When I was a trainee reporter in Kent ('where I doubt not is spoken as broad and rude English as in any place in England' – William Caxton), one of our first lessons was how to spell and pronounce local placenames: Loose (pronounced *Looze*, fortunately for Loose women), Meopham (pronounced *Meppam*), Trottiscliffe (pronounced *Trosley*), and so on. You could, of course, pronounce these places however you liked, and local people would probably know what you meant – but you found out how they did it, and followed suit, if you wanted to be taken seriously and not look silly. Much the same applies to correct spelling, as my local paper found out in 2013 when it reported: 'Electric trains can accelerate and break more quickly.' Or when the *Guardian*, in a report about Syria, referred to 'a barbed-wife fence'.

In 1750, Lord Chesterfield wrote to his son: 'I must tell you, that orthography, in the true sense of the word, is so absolutely necessary for a man of letters, or a gentleman, that one false spelling may fix a ridicule upon him for the rest of his life; and I know a man of quality, who never recovered the ridicule of having spelled *wholesome* without the *w*.' Five years later Samuel Johnson's dictionary was published. English orthography (the right way to spell words) had fluctuated wildly until then – the printer William Caxton couldn't decide whether to print the word for 'eggs' as *egges* or *eyren*, since both were in use in the late 15th century – but has been pretty constant ever since.

English spelling is not as complicated as it is made out to be but it is not phonetic, which has led to various attempts to 'simplify' it. The main reason they have failed – with a few exceptions when Noah Webster compiled the first American dictionary and changed *centre* to *center* and *colour* to *color* – is that English is spoken in so many different ways. Just think of all the accents and dialects in the UK, the US, and many other countries where English is either a native language or at least widely spoken. Who would decide how 'simplified' words should be spelt? Unlike written English, there is no standard form of spoken English.

George Bernard Shaw, who fought an endearingly barking campaign for *bomb* to be spelt 'bom' – what he would have done about 'chocolate bombe' is not recorded – proposed establishing an entirely new alphabet. Such reformers are missing the point, which is that they would never be able to satisfy all the different varieties of English. To take one example, as a northerner I am proud to pronounce *bath* as it was in Old English, with a short vowel sound as in 'cat'; my wife, who hails from the fine Surrey town of Godalming, pronounces it with the more recent southern long vowel sound as in 'cart'. How would it be spelt 'rationally'? Then there is *scone*, which can be pronounced to rhyme with 'gone' or 'loan' (and 'soon', if you include the Scone where Robert the Bruce was crowned). Would a spelling reformer choose scon, skon, scoan, skoan, scoon or skoon?

English has a widely used vowel sound (the schwa, like the second A in *magazine*), which cannot be 'spelt' at all except

---

@3duser Some basic help with capitals, please.
Is it 'Captain Bloggs' and 'the captain'?

when using the phonetic alphabet. Pronunciation differences become more, er, pronounced when English is spoken overseas, but however differently people speak it, written English is intelligible throughout the English-speaking world – just as written Chinese is the same for Mandarin and Cantonese speakers who can't understand what each other are saying. So, I am afraid, those who would like to go back to pronouncing the K in *knee*, as was the practice in Middle English, or spelling it 'nee', are likely to be disappointed.

How difficult is English spelling? David Crystal says in *The English Language* that there are only 400 or so everyday English words whose spelling is wholly irregular. What's more, he suggests, you can learn the rules: for example, when adding *-ing* to a verb that ends in a consonant, you double the last letter if the verb has a short vowel (thus *bet* becomes *betting*), but don't double it if the vowel is long (so *beat* becomes *beating*). I wouldn't fancy trying to teach this to a class of eight-year-olds, but I'm not a teacher. I wonder if you wouldn't be better off just learning the irregular words, as we did in Mrs Birtles' class, although some of her advice turned out to be deeply suspect – for example, 'I before E except after C'. It's a miracle I can spell *deign, feign, heir, species* and *weird*.

One tip, though, if you are not sure how to spell a word. (And you don't have a computer or phone with a spellchecker to hand. And there is no dictionary within reach.) Have a look at the morphology (word structure) by breaking it down into its component parts. Take *supercalifragilisticexpialidocious*. Even though the sound of it is something quite atrocious, it's not hard to spell if you split it up into sections: super-cali-fragil-istic-expi-ali-docious. You can do

@guardianstyle Yes, but the Captain and Tenille.

the same with anti-dis-establish-ment-ari-an-ism and other long words. But, sadly, no system can help you decide how many Cs and Ms there are in *accommodation* (two of each). You just have to learn it.

Here are some words that lots of people, including me, have trouble with.

abattoir: one B, two Ts.

abscess: S, C in the middle.

absorb: but **absorption**.

acknowledgement: E after the G.

aficionado: one F.

appal: one L; but it really is **appalling** two Ls.

barbecue: in *Troublesome Words*, Bill Bryson writes: 'Barbecue is the only acceptable spelling in serious writing. Any journalist or other formal user of English who believes that the word is spelled *barbeque* or, worse still, *bar-b-q* is not ready for unsupervised employment.' The capitalised versions, *B-B-Q* and *BBQ* (as favoured by, you won't be surprised to learn, Tesco) are no less objectionable.

berserk: two Rs.

....

@n0aaa So on a CV: worked with the director of Human Resources?

cemetery: not cemetary, and certainly not Pet Sematary.

choose: two Os; **chose** one O. Perhaps a typing rather than spelling mistake – although I see it a lot, often from people who make the same mistake with **loose** and **lose**.

committee: two Ms, two Ts.

consensus: not concensus.

desiccated: one S, two Cs, even if you don't think it looks right.

develop: not develope (despite envelope).

diphtheria, **diphthong**: not diptheria, dipthong.

distil: one L.

drunkenness: two Ns, two Ss.

embarrassment: two Rs, two Ss.

exorbitant: no H.

fine-tooth comb: not 'fine tooth-comb'.

fuchsia: not fuschia. It may help to remember that it was named after a botanist called Fuchs.

fulfil: one L at the end.

@guardianstyle No, it looks awful; human resources is fine.

guttural: (nothing to do with gutters).

haemorrhage, **haemorrhaging**. **haemorrhoids**

harass, **harassment**: one R, two Ss.

harebrained: not hairbrained.

hitchhiker: two Hs.

humour: but **humorous**.

idiosyncrasy, **idiosyncrasies**: not idiosyncracy, idiosyncracies.

impostor: not imposter. A very common error.

independent: not independant.

inoculate: one N.

install, **instalment**: one L only in the latter.

instil: one L.

liaise, **liaison**: watch those Is.

linchpin: not lynchpin. Even if they spell it right, most people are unaware that it is a pin that keeps a wheel in place on its axle.

@anthonylydgate Fidel Castros, or Fidels Castro?

liquefy: not liquify.

manoeuvring: unlike **manoeuvre**, no E after the V and R. One I always have to look up.

millennium: two Ls, two Ns.

minuscule: not miniscule.

mischievous: not mischievious.

mis-hit, **mis-sell**, **misspell**, **misspent**: easily misspelt.

no one: no hyphen.

ophthalmologist: not opthalmologist.

possess, possession: two Ss, twice.

privilege: two Is, then an E.

publicly: not publically.

quandary: not quandry.

questionnaire: two Ns, unlike commissionaire.

rarefied: not rarified.

receive: not recieve.

@guardianstyle Fidel Castros (plural).
'He out-Fidel Castroed Fidel Castro' (verb).

recommendation: one C, two Ms.

restaurateur: not restauranteur.

rhythm: not rhythym.

sacrilegious: not sacreligious.

separate: not seperate.

septuagenarian: with a U.

seize: is sometimes wrongly spelt sieze, perhaps by people taught the 'I before E' rule.

sequined: one N.

shoo-in: not shoe-in.

siege: is sometimes wrongly spelt seige, perhaps a result of confusion with seize.

skilful: not skilfull, skillful or skillfull.

sleight: of hand, not slight.

stupefied: not stupified.

supersede: not supercede.

@3duser Snuck or sneaked?

under way: not underway.

vichyssoise: three Ss. If you are unsure, call it leek and potato soup.

weird: not wierd. E before I again.

withhold: two Hs.

People and Places

> *When I see my name spelt with one word, I want to slap and choke people. If you do that, you got to be a moron … It's on every poster, every album and every ticket as two words. If you spell it as one, you're an idiot. Bottom line.*
> MEAT LOAF

As 'the Loaf' avers, there is no excuse for getting someone's name wrong, especially when we now have something called the world wide web where you can check spellings of proper names very easily. A few of the most common errors, which I have come across again and again, and still keep coming across, are:

Thomas **Becket**. Not 'à Becket'.

Colombia the country does not have a U in it, unlike **Columbia University** and **District of Columbia**. They are all named after Christopher Columbus, or Cristoforo Colombo as he was known in his native Italy.

EE Cummings, not 'ee cummings'. He may not have used capitals in his poems, but he used them in his name.

Judi Dench, not Judy.

Lucian Freud, not Lucien.

Ivory Coast, **Lebanon**, **Ukraine**, no 'the'.

Johns Hopkins University not John Hopkins, and **Stanford University** not Stamford.

Kirkcaldy, not Kirkaldy, is in **Fife**, not Fyfe.

Liechtenstein the country, not to be confused with Roy **Lichtenstein** the late pop artist.

Mary Celeste. The boat whose crew mysteriously disappeared in the middle of the Atlantic in 1872 is spelt thus, and not Marie Celeste. I hope to live long enough to see someone spell it correctly, but I am not optimistic.

Middle-earth, not Middle Earth.

Moby-Dick, with a hyphen.

Middlesbrough, not Middlesborough, is in **Teesside**, not Teeside. Bill Bryson describes the former as 'probably the

@JulieRoffABC Literature, wit, pedantry & musical theatre. You are SO my kind of people.

most misspelled community name in Britain' and the latter as 'possibly the most commonly misspelled geographical designation in Britain'.

An A–Z of Interesting and Occasionally Useful Stuff about Words

A is for Abbreviations
Words are abbreviated in four ways:

- acronyms, which use the initials to spell out a word (for example, Nato, laser);
- initialisms (pm, PMT);
- contractions (Dr, won't); and
- shortenings (phone, etc).

If you want to know what they all stand for, *Alphabet Soup* is a useful reference book published by Bloomsbury in 2004. It lists more than 8,000 abbreviations but disappointingly omits to mention mofo, ROFL or Spam. It does, however, include HP (hire purchase), a form of commerce last used in about 1959, and LMKOWOTO, which it describes as 'used in e-mails' to mean 'let me know one way or the other', a claim I find improbable.

Talking of messy food, most British newspapers don't use full stops after abbreviations and do use lowercase for acronyms – Aids rather than AIDS, Unesco rather than UNESCO, and so on. The aim is to prevent their pages resembling a plate of Alphabetti Spaghetti.

B is for Buffalo

Buffalo buffalo Buffalo buffalo buffalo buffalo Buffalo buffalo.
Antanaclasis is the rhetorical term for repeating a word in a different sense, as in this perfectly grammatical sentence. If you know that Buffalo is a US city, buffalo can be a verb meaning to bully, and of course buffalo are animals, then you can read it correctly to mean, with an explanation in square brackets: 'Buffalo [place] buffalo [animals] / [whom] Buffalo [place] buffalo [animals] buffalo [bully] / [do in turn] buffalo [bully] Buffalo [place] buffalo [animals].'

Readers who were paying attention to chapter 1 will have worked out that, syntactically, the subject of the main clause of this sentence is *Buffalo buffalo*; *Buffalo buffalo buffalo* is a relative clause; the main verb is – you guessed it – *buffalo*; and the direct object is *Buffalo buffalo*.

Shakespeare used this form of play on words frequently, as in 'to England will I steal, and there I'll steal' (*Henry V*). Headline and advertising copywriters are also fond of the device, not to be confused with the similar epizeuxis, which also relies on repetition, as in 'Thou'lt come no more, Never, never, never, never, never!' (*King Lear*), 'Good morning, good morning, good' (the Beatles), and 'Good morning, good morning, good morning, good morning' (Kanye West).

C is for Capital Letters

Some words need capitals for legal reasons, including trademarks such as Jacuzzi, Lego and Portakabin, a company whose lawyers will send you threatening letters if you refer to a 'portaloo' without checking thoroughly whether it is, in fact, an authentic high-quality all-steel portable toilet made

@crypticcricket Is it said 'B-oh-ee' or 'B-ow-ee'?
I've never been sure.

by them, as used by the Manic Street Preachers, in which case it's a Portaloo. The same applies to food given the European Commission's 'protected geographical indication' (PGI) status, such as Cornish pasties and clotted cream, Melton Mowbray pork pies, and Parma ham. This is why Gorgonzola cheese has a capital letter but cheddar cheese (which is made all over the place, not just in Cheddar) doesn't. An exception to this rule is champagne, which has protected status but which no one capitalises. So far as I am aware, this doesn't seem to bother anyone in Champagne.

The list of words based on proper names that have largely lost connection with their origins, and which therefore are not – or do not need to be – capitalised, is a long one that includes *balaclava, boycott, caesar salad, cardigan, chauvinist, french fries, french horn, french kiss, french letter, french polish, french toast* and *french windows, leotard, lynching, sandwich* and *wellington boots*. The *Guardian* has been spelling Yorkshire pudding 'yorkshire pudding' for 50 years, probably just to annoy Yorkshiremen.

A couple of years ago, New York City decided to replace 250,000 street signs in capital letters with new signs that just capitalise the initial letter (eg, Broadway instead of BROADWAY) on the grounds that studies show it is harder to read all-capital signs and they can cause accidents, particularly among older drivers, because of the extra milliseconds spent looking away from the road. The decision echoed one taken in the UK 50 years ago, when the designers Jock Kinneir and Margaret Calvert were given the task of updating the country's chaotic system of road signs. They concluded that 'a combination of upper and lowercase letters would be more legible than conventional uppercase lettering'. The classic signage they designed is still in use.

In the 18th century it became fashionable to spell all nouns with a capital letter. Local Authorities, Estate Agents and Germans continue the Practice today. I'm no great fan of capitals but you can go too far. The South African poet Antjie Krog wrote: 'I am a poet: I distrust anything that starts with a capital letter and ends with a full stop.'

Capital letters are useful for avoiding ambiguity in such sentences as: 'The most interesting character in *Borgen* is Bent.'

D is for Doshes

Or should that be *distims*? Both, in fact. Andrew Ingraham (1841–1905) – one of my heroes, although hardly anyone has heard of him – was a headmaster of Swain School in Massachusetts, which offered free courses to students who otherwise would not have been able to afford higher education. He also came up with the 'Gostak concept' in the phrase 'the gostak distims the doshes', an example of how one derives meaning from the syntax of a sentence even if it is semantically meaningless. The idea is that without knowing what it means, an English speaker would recognise *the gostak* as a noun phrase and the subject of the sentence, *distims* as a verb, and *the doshes* as another noun phrase and the object of the sentence.

The concept is similar to, if less sophisticated than, the much better known sentence composed by Noam Chomsky in *Syntactic Structures* (1957): 'Colorless green ideas sleep furiously', which he contrasted with 'Furiously sleep ideas green colorless', pointing out that the first is nonsensical but grammatical, while the second is nonsensical and ungram-

---

@SirVaylo Your take on 'high call volumes';
that expression so beloved of call centre operatives?

matical. Unlike Ingraham, he used real rather than invented words to demonstrate that human speech does not follow statistical models: his grammatical sentence remained so even if no one had ever uttered it.

E is for Eskimo

Eskimo is a language spoken in Greenland, Canada, Alaska and Siberia. The people are Inuit (singular Inuk), not 'Eskimos'. As everyone knows, they have more than 100 words for snow. Everyone is wrong. Phil James produced a list of all 100. They include *tlalman* (snow sold to German tourists), *mextla* (snow used to make Eskimo margaritas), and *MacTla* (snow burgers). It's a spoof. Nonetheless you still find writers repeating this cliche all the time, the result of a well-meaning – but inaccurate and patronising – attempt in the early 20th century to show that Inuit culture and language were as sophisticated as those of America.

This brings me on to snowclones, which derive their name from this very factoid. Geoffrey Pullum, who wrote an essay called 'The Great Eskimo Vocabulary Hoax', defines a snowclone as 'a multi-use, customisable, instantly recognisable, timeworn, quoted or misquoted phrase or sentence that can be used in an entirely open array of different variants'. A good example of a snowclone is 'X is the new Y' (where X might be comedy, and Y rock'n'roll; but X might equally be Torquay, and Y Tuscany). Another example: 'You wait ages for an X, and then Y come along all at once' (X are most commonly London buses, but could be gold medals or anything else, and Y is typically three but can be any number). See any newspaper for further examples. Such phrases are very popular with journalists searching for what Pullum calls 'quick-fix ways of writing stuff without actually having to think out new descriptive vocabulary or construct new phrases and sentences'.

F is for Famously

If something is famous, you shouldn't need to say so; famously is even worse. Journalists use it to mean one of two things, both irritating:

> *I know everyone already knows this, but I can't think of an original way to start so I am going to say it anyway …*

as in 'Harold Macmillan, asked what the biggest challenge is for any leader, famously replied: "Events, my dear boy, events."'

> *You don't know this? I do. That shows I am clever and know lots of stuff you don't …*

as in 'Reich famously declined to continue in academia, preferring to support himself via a series of blue-collar jobs'.

G is for Gategate

The five men who broke into Democratic party HQ in the Watergate building in Washington DC in 1972 brought down a president and started a tradition of adding the suffix *gate* to any major, or minor, scandal. Sir Alex Ferguson alone has featured in at least three (Fingergate, Piegate and Pizzagate). In the world of sport, we have had Beachballgate,

---

@ben_jarman brussels sprouts or Brussels sprouts?

Bloodgate, Buttongate, Chicanegate, Crashgate, Henrygate (also known as Handgate or Thierrygate), Liargate, Tevezgate and, of course, Tigergate. Other examples range from the mildly droll (Gatecrashergate, Henry Gatesgate, also known as Stupidgate) to the pathetic (Sexy Photo Gate).

Among dozens of others are Bertiegate, Betsygate, Billygate, Camillagate (not to be confused with Dianagate, also known as Squidgygate), Chcriegate, Fajitagate, at least two Grannygates, Hobnobgate, Irangate, Iraqgate, Monicagate, Plebgate, Sachsgate, various Strippergates, Terrygate, Toiletgate, three different cases of Troopergate, and Whitewatergate. You could argue that occasionally this device is a useful way to pull a lot of material together under one heading; Climategate, perhaps. Mainly, it's silly. As Mitchell and Webb had it:

> *'What would you call a scandal about water?'*
> *'Aquagate.'*

Personally, I think it's time to shut the gate.

H is for Hyphens

If not an endangered species, hyphens in compound words are certainly in decline. Prefixes such as macro, mega, micro, mini, multi, over, super and under rarely need them. Many people, including me, think they clutter up text (particularly when your computer breaks already hyphenated words at the end of a line) and look old-fashioned. In his *Introduction to the Grammar of English* Rodney Huddleston, in his inimitable style, writes: 'The transition from space to hyphen to close juxtaposition reflects the progressive institutionalisation of the compound.' He means the process where electronic mail, for example, became E mail, E-mail or e-mail before completing its inevitable journey to become one word. This happens as concepts become more familiar – words such as boy-friend, head-master, house-wife, wire-less and up-stairs used to be hyphenated. If you continue to spell them as two words, or with a hyphen, you will look un-cool.

Where hyphens are essential is to avoid ambiguity, especially with compound adjectives: a hyphen is the difference between a man eating squid and a man-eating squid. Civil rights movement and financial services sector don't need hyphens, but black-cab driver does to avoid confusion with black cab-driver. A missing hyphen in a *Guardian* review of Chekhov's *Three Sisters* led us to refer to 'the servant abusing Natasha' rather than 'the servant-abusing Natasha'. You don't need to hyphenate adverbs, either – they look ugly in phrases such as hotly disputed penalty, genetically modified crops, etc – unless, again, it's to avoid ambiguity: an ill-prepared person is not the same as an ill, prepared one.

Verbs also need hyphens sometimes to stop this kind of thing happening:

> *Motorists*
> *told: don't*
> *panic buy*
> *petrol*

Perhaps my colleague panic-wrote this but it is ambiguous: you just have to guess whether it means 'Don't panic. Buy petrol' (advice given by a government minister in 2012) or

@matt–fwyalchen Do you think you will have less enquiries over Christmas?

'Don't panic-buy petrol' (advice more typically given, and ignored, by government ministers during fuel shortages).

Some people worry about whether to hyphenate words beginning with *re*. The rule is use *re-* (with hyphen) when followed by E or U (not pronounced as 'yu'), as in *re-entry*, *re-examine*, *re-urge*; use *re* (no hyphen) when followed by A, I, O or U (pronounced as 'yu'), or a consonant, as in *rearm*, *rearrange*, *reiterate*, *reorder*, *reuse*, *retweet*. Also use a hyphen to avoid ambiguity, as when someone *re-signs*, rather than *resigns*.

I is for Idioms

An idiom is an expression that adds up to more than the sum of its parts – you can't predict what it means, or can do so only vaguely, from the meanings of the words it contains. Idioms present problems for people learning a foreign language. A student of English who has learned the meaning of 'he kicked the ball' would not get very far with 'he kicked the bucket' (unless someone literally did kick a bucket). At mealtimes, an idiom is the difference between a hot dog and a red herring. The syntax and semantics of idioms are rather strange: you might say 'Dom spilled the beans' if he betrayed a secret, but not 'Dom spilled the secret beans'.

However, idioms are not totally random. Many grammarians studying the 'realm of idiomaticity' say it includes much that is highly structured and consistent. For example, you can keep your cool, blow your cool, or lose your cool. You might be able to guess the meaning of some idioms (close shave) or even work out from the context what they mean (pulling the strings; you can't make an omelette without breaking eggs). A survey of 75 idioms from a 50-million-word corpus of *Guardian* and *Wall Street Journal* stories established that 64 of them had been modified: call the tune became 'call the political tune', keep tabs on became 'keep ecological tabs on', and so on. Idioms can also be reinvented, or at least updated, as when mutton dressed as lamb became 'Whitney dressed as Britney'. The linguist Ray Jackendoff, with the help of his 11-year-old daughter, studied the American TV quiz *Wheel of Fortune*, in which contestants have to guess words and phrases. He estimated that people carry a mental store of up to 25,000 such expressions.

Every language has them: French people can suffer from *un chat à la gorge* (a cat, rather than a frog, in the throat) and their version of playing gooseberry is the much more evocative *tenir la chandelle* (hold the candle): the image is of an unwelcome third party on a date holding a candle for the two lovers. And according to the BBC programme *QI*, the Greeks have a phrase – *Katatraya stayeftika* – that means something like 'who gives a shit?' but literally translates as 'there is trouble in the Gypsy village'.

I have been unable to find out, however, why in English we say six of one, half a dozen of the other but not 12 of one, a dozen of the other.

J is for Just Deserts

Not 'just desserts', unless you are saying that you will forgo the steak and chips in return for a double helping of death by chocolate. This is a very common error, presumably because they are pronounced the same. *Deserts* in this sense are something you deserve. Both words are derived from Latin via similar French verbs: *deservir* (deserve) and *desservir* (clear the table).

K is for Knockout

It's one word for a noun ('a first-round knockout') or adjective ('a knockout blow'). The verb is two words ('Colin "Bomber" Harris has knocked himself out'; 'they knocked out hundreds of counterfeit DVDs'). This pattern is very common in English. Other examples include: *bailout* and *bail out*, *kickoff* and *kick off*, *lineup* and *line up*, *sellout* and *sell out*, *startup* and *start up*. Some people might hyphenate the nouns and adjectives ('knock-out' and so on), but not if they were paying attention to the entry above on hyphens.

L is for Literally

> *Everything that happens, happens literally. If it doesn't, then it literally didn't happen.*
>
> KEITH WATERHOUSE

Can *literally* be used to mean figuratively? Clearly it can and is, notably by sports commentators. Jamie Redknapp is fluent in the language of the literal: crosses are 'literally on a plate', a team are 'literally passed to death', a player 'literally hasn't got a right foot' and the fans 'literally go insane'. But Charles Dickens and James Joyce used *literally* metaphorically too, as did Saul Bellow who wrote 'The earth is literally a mirror of thoughts'. The general idea seems to be to add emphasis ('Yeah, I dropped the "literally" bomb,' as my colleague Hadley Freeman put it), although the writer Ben Masters suggests: 'Maybe we're a generation that is scared of commitment ... Maybe our misuse reveals a deeper insecurity about what in fact is real.' Many grammarians have no problem with this as they see it as just another example of language change. To me it seems perverse to use a word to mean something like its opposite. The literal meaning of *literally* can be quite useful – 'I've literally not eaten all day' means you are ravenous, not that you feel a bit peckish. Figurative use of the word may also distract the reader by sounding comical, as in 'United literally came back from the dead' or 'he literally exploded into action'.

M is for Modal

Modality has preoccupied philosophers for thousands of years. Modal logic concerns notions of necessity and possibility and what might be – or might have been – rather than what actually is. In grammar, modal meaning can be signalled by verbs such as assume, believe, demand or insist; adverbs such as definitely, maybe, allegedly or perhaps; and the modal auxiliary verbs that give people so much trouble: may, might, must, can, could, will, would, shall, should, need, ought and dare.

There are two types of modality. One, *deontic*, concerns the speaker's view of how people should behave ('you must leave now'); the other, *epistemic*, reflects the speaker's judgment about the truth of what they say ('you must be Dr Livingstone'). Native English speakers will be aware of the subtle distinctions between, say, 'I could have been a contender' (but I'm not), 'I should have been a contender' (I wish I had), 'I would have been a contender' (if the fight hadn't been fixed), and so on. They are much harder for people learning English to grasp.

An odd characteristic of modal verbs is that past tense forms (might, could, would) can be used to represent present and future: 'I might call you next week' and 'would you come

@abhistruse Mail from twitter: 'Here are accounts similar to who you followed.' Shouldn't it be 'to whom'?

up and see me some time?' have nothing to do with the past. In practice, they are sometimes ambiguous: 'this appliance must be earthed' could be an instruction to earth it or an opinion that it already has been.

The boundaries between modal verbs are blurring. Most people would perceive little or no difference between 'it may rain tomorrow' and 'it might rain tomorrow'. I've written headlines where we changed *might* to *may* not because of the meaning but because *might* didn't fit. There is a subtle difference, however. 'May' can imply that something has happened: 'Goal-line technology may have changed football for ever' (Fifa has introduced it). Whereas 'might' suggests it hasn't: 'Goal-line technology might have changed the result of the 1966 World Cup final' (if it had existed). Note the difference too between 'they may have played tennis, or they may have gone boating' (I don't know) and 'they might have played tennis, or they might have gone boating' (but they didn't, because it's raining).

The *Guardian* headline 'Capello has stayed aloof but personal touch may have kept Bridge onside' says the opposite of what is meant – it suggests that Capello's personal touch means there is still a possibility of Bridge staying onside; it should have read 'Capello has stayed aloof but personal touch might have kept Bridge onside' (but it didn't).

Just to complicate things further, 'may' also has the meaning of having permission: 'Murdoch may bid for Sky' could mean he is considering a bid, or the competition authorities have allowed him to.

Perhaps because people are too busy to worry about such details, use of all the modal auxiliaries except *can* and *could* has declined over the last few decades.

@guardianstyle No, 'to those'.

N is for Names

Tony Digweed, of Newbury in Berkshire, got so fed up with jokes about his name that he decided to take up digging weeds as a career and is now a professional gardener. This is an extreme case of 'nominative determinism', a phenomenon normally associated with mild coincidences (such as a locksmith, let's say, being called Mr Key), and satirised by this brilliant *Guardian* reader's letter: 'At a London hospital where I worked, there was a surgeon Cutting, a haematologist Blud, a Chinese dentist Fang, an orthopaedic surgeon Limb, a Dr Nurse and a nurse Doctor – whom I confusingly introduced to each other at a party ... A local GP was Dr De'Ath, a Chinese junior psychiatrist Dr So Wat ... ' and so on. This seems a good moment to mention the fact that Thomas Crapper, although a plumber, did not invent the water closet and did not give his name to what it is used for.

Funny names, however, are very effective in fiction. Charles Dickens found just the right name for a remarkable array of characters, from Josiah Bounderby and Serjeant Buzfuz to Wackford Squeers and Poll Sweedlepipe. His Winkle, Wopsie and Wititterly would have been at home alongside WC Boggs, Dr Carver and Marshall P Nutt in the *Carry On* films, while Anne Chickenstalker sounds like a Monty Python character. The Python team took the joke about as far as it could go with the Silly party election candidate Tarquin Fin-tim-lin-bin-whin-bim-lim Bus Stop F'tang F'tang Olé Biscuitbarrel, then venturing to the outer limits of surreal nomenclature with a character whose name mainly comprised extracts from pop songs and sound effects.

@shaunrowlandb Your thoughts on starting sentences with 'however'?

Roald Dahl, who delighted young readers of *Charlie and the Chocolate Factory* with characters such as Augustus Gloop, Veruca Salt and Mike Teavee, told a story in his 1986 autobiography about a journey to Africa by ship in which a fellow passenger was so sensitive about his baldness that he carried a secret selection of wigs and sprinkled Epsom salts on his jacket to simulate dandruff. The funniest part of the anecdote is that this person was called, or so Dahl claims, UN Savory. No one apart from me seems to have challenged the veracity of this tale but I have always been struck by its resemblance to Graham Greene's 1932 novel *Stamboul Train*, in which an absurd, pompous character heading east – though by rail, rather than sea – is called QC Savory. Perhaps Dahl was playing a little joke on posterity.

O is for Omnishambles
A case of life imitating art. Oxford Dictionaries' word of the year for 2012 – a late tweak to a script for a 2009 episode of the BBC political satire *The Thick of It* – became indelibly associated with the coalition government. Particularly after the 2012 budget, in which George Osborne contrived to upset churchgoers, grandmothers and people who eat Cornish pasties. The chancellor was not alone: a visit to Britain by Mitt Romney, the Republican candidate for US president, quickly turned into a 'Romneyshambles'.

@guardianstyle However you look at it, it's fine. However, note comma.

P is for *Paradise Lost*

> *Of Mans First Disobedience, and the Fruit*
> *Of that Forbidden Tree, whose mortal tast*
> *Brought Death into the World, and all our woe,*
> *With loss of EDEN, till one greater Man*
> *Restore us, and regain the blissful Seat,*
> *Sing Heav'nly Muse ...*

JOHN MILTON, *PARADISE LOST*

Fighting your way to the sixth line before you get to the verb *sing* is hard work; it is known as fronting or topicalisation, a device of which Milton, like Yoda, was fond. When he writes 'Yet one tree you must not touch' (rather than 'You must not touch one tree'), the effect is dramatic: by changing the usual English subject-verb-object order, he shifts the emphasis of the message to the tree in the Garden of Eden. *Paradise Lost* also introduced to the world the enduringly evocative phrase 'all Hell broke loose'.

I imagine very few people read Milton these days, and had we been offered a choice my English A-level class would have cheerfully opted to have our fingernails extracted as an alternative to studying *Samson Agonistes*. Set to music, however, it's a different story: a Mark Morris Dance Group performance of *L'Allegro, Il Penseroso ed Il Moderato* (music: Handel, lyrics: Milton) at the Edinburgh festival in the early 1990s remains the most magical night I have spent in any theatre.

Q is for Quixotic

This word means naively idealistic, like Don Quixote in Miguel de Cervantes' *The Ingenious Gentleman Don Quixote of La Mancha*, not just vaguely eccentric. Although the novel was published in two parts, in 1605 and 1615, the first use of the word in English listed in the OED is from the satirist Nicholas Amhurst's *Protestant Popery* in 1718: 'Pulpit and Press fictitious Ills engage, And combat Windmills with Quixotic Rage.' Some things don't change.

R is for RP

Nothing to do with Standard English, which addresses the need for an agreed set of rules that can be taught in reading and writing, RP (received pronunciation) refers only to how words are pronounced. At one time, a West Country accent was the most prestigious in England; strange to think that the Wurzels would have been regarded as posher than, say, Joan Bakewell. RP was established as prestigious as recently as the late 19th century and was not called that until the 1920s. Few people use it – perhaps 2 per cent of the population – and it is a social rather than a regional accent: if you went to a 'public' (private) school anywhere in England, it is how you probably speak. RP is a class thing, which is why it's also known as 'BBC English', 'Oxford English' or 'the Queen's English', although it is no longer much of an advantage to speak it. Many call centres favour Scottish accents and northerners have been tolerated by the BBC since Wilfred Pickles (a Yorkshireman who was very popular with my grandparents' generation) was allowed to read the news during the second world war because it was felt that his accent would confuse the Nazis.

@guardianstyle A frequently asked question is an FAQ.

RP is, however, still taught to foreigners learning English. There is no logical reason why they should learn RP rather than, say, estuary English, which scholars have noted contains some of the features of RP, is spoken by many more people, and does not make you sound like a Tory twit. This may explain why George Osborne, the chancellor, suddenly started speaking Mockney in 2013. Not everyone approves of such developments: when Nasser Hussain was appointed England cricket captain, the *Daily Telegraph*'s comment was: 'Somebody who went to a good university has no excuse for speaking in that ghastly estuary sludge.'

S is for Shibboleth

> *And the Gileadites took the passages of Jordan before the Ephraimites: and it was so, that when those Ephraimites which were escaped said, Let me go over; that the men of Gilead said unto him, Art thou an Ephraimite? If he said, Nay;*
> *Then said they unto him, Say now Shibboleth: and he said Sibboleth: for he could not frame to pronounce it right. Then they took him, and slew him at the passages of Jordan: and there fell at that time of the Ephraimites forty and two thousand.*
>
> JUDGES 12:5–6 (AUTHORISED VERSION)

This gruesome tale is reminiscent of the heyday of football violence in the 1970s, when it was the custom among fans of some clubs (Leeds United and Chelsea spring to mind) to ask

---

@davidsw19 Why is auntie a proper noun?

someone the time, and if their pronunciation differed from the local norm, 'kick their head in'.

The economist Paul Samuelson applied the word *shibboleth* to an idea for which 'the means becomes the end, and the letter of the law takes precedence over the spirit', and some linguists use it in this sense to mean pedantic adherence to a supposed law of language that never applied, or no longer does, such as the 'rules' discussed in chapter 2.

Steven Pinker writes in *The Language Instinct*: 'Since prescriptive rules are so psychologically unnatural that only those with access to the right schooling can abide by them, they serve as shibboleths, differentiating the elite from the rabble.'

T is for Trousers

Everyone knows the difference between lambs (cute) and lamb (good with mint sauce), but to a linguist the distinction is between the countable and uncountable reference of the noun *lamb*. People interested in such matters also wonder: are trousers singular or plural? The grammarian HA Gleason tells the story of a man asked this question whose reply was: 'Well, mine are plural at the bottom, and singular at the top.' Gleason thinks it is entirely arbitrary that English grammar regards them as plural. The Polish semanticist Anna Wierzbicka argues that there is nothing arbitrary about it at all, and that words behave the way they do because they are governed by subtle semantic rules. Trousers, like tights, scissors, binoculars and forceps, belong to a category of objects with two identical parts, joined together and performing the same function. Or as she puts it: native English speakers

@guardianstyle You wouldn't capitalise my Auntie Joan, say? You don't want to upset Auntie Joan.

regard trousers as 'saliently bipartite'. Which is why Ken and Kenneth, the 'suit you, sir' tailors in *The Fast Show*, were so funny when they referred to 'a good trouser, sir'.

Wierzbicka is a fascinating linguist. In 1972 she produced a list of 14 'semantic primitives' that she believed form the universal base of all human thought. They were:

- want;
- don't want;
- feel;
- think of;
- imagine;
- say;
- become;
- be a part of;
- something;
- someone;
- I;
- you;
- world; and
- this.

She cut the list to 13 five years later, expanded it to 37 in 1993, then decided this was 'unrealistically small' and increased it again in 1996 to 55.

Getting back to trousers, is it 'all mouth and trousers' or 'all mouth and no trousers'? The 'no' was probably a later addition, although both expressions work perfectly well to describe someone who promises much but fails to deliver. Michael Quinion's excellent book *Port Out, Starboard Home*

@journoraven Why is it 'cow meat' and 'pig meat' but 'horsemeat'?

(Penguin, 2005) says: 'All mouth and trousers: this strange expression comes from the north of England and is used, mainly by women in my experience, as a sharp-tongued and effective putdown of a certain kind of pushy, over-confident male. It's a wonderful example of metonymy ("a container for the thing contained").' Idioms that express the same general idea include the American English 'all hat [or big hat] and no cattle' and the French *il ne pisse pas loin*.

U is for Unique
Purists will get upset and denounce you on Twitter if you qualify this word and similar absolutes, although Charlotte Brontë used 'very unique' and Kingsley Amis says that 'rather unique' is acceptable if you mean unique in some ways, but not in others. Likewise, 'almost invariably' means hardly ever changing and if anyone says you can't use it like that, tell them you almost invariably do.

V is for Vagueness
Bertrand Russell was much preoccupied with this concept, going so far as to invent his own language because he found English too vague. Linguists and philosophers have spent centuries debating categories: Ludwig Wittgenstein and others have mused over what comprises the essence of a chair and whether, for example, a mug is a kind of cup or whether a robin is a more prototypical bird than a turkey. Aristotle thought everything could be defined precisely and William Blake said 'a good Apple tree or a Bad, is an Apple tree still', but these days boundaries are widely considered fuzzy. So in grammar, *happily* is regarded as a prototypical

adverb but *abroad* isn't. If I sound a bit vague about this, I am only following Russell's advice: 'In the words of the poet, who speaks of vagueness should himself be vague.' He didn't say which poet.

W is for Welch

If you want to annoy a Welsh person, accuse them of 'welshing' on an agreement. Actually, they won't be that happy if you accuse them of 'welching', but at least you will have spelt it correctly. Similarly, it's the Welch Regiment (or was, until 1969) and the Royal Welch Fusiliers (until 2006). Welsh rarebit, not rabbit, is 'posh cheese on toast' according to the Hairy Bikers. Finally, never call Wales a principality, or try to calculate how many times it would fit into Lake Titicaca.

X is for Xmas

Regarded by some as vulgar, even blasphemous, although the word Christmas itself is a contraction of 'Christ's mass'. Long before Slade wished us 'Merry Xmas Everybody', Coleridge was writing to Southey, on Christmas Eve 1799, to tell him: 'My Xstmas [sic] Carol is a quaint performance' and in 1884 the magazine *Punch* even used 'Xmassing' as a verb. It's very useful in single-column headlines.

Y is for Yours

Confusion between *your*, *you're* and *yours* is almost as widespread as between *their*, *they're*, *theirs* and *there's*. Both examples illustrate why I argue that 'possessive' is not a very helpful term when you are trying to decide whether to use

---

@guardianstyle Have seen and heard a lot of '... since the war ...' today. If they mean 'second world war', can they tell us please?

an apostrophe. Remember that with pronouns you need one only if something has been missed out, which takes care of *you're* ('you are') and *they're* ('they are'), as well as *there's* ('there is'). You may say that *your* (as in 'your book') and *yours* (as in 'is this book yours?') are surely possessive, as are *their* and *theirs* – and you would be right – but I promise you that *yours* and *theirs*, like *his* and *hers*, do not have an apostrophe.

Z is for Zeugma

Zeugma (ancient Greek for yoke) is a figure of speech in which, typically, a single verb is used to yoke together two or more parts of a sentence with different meanings, as in 'Mr Pickwick took his hat and his leave'. My favourite example is this gem in the *Guardian* by Ronald Bergan in his 2010 obituary of June Havoc, Gypsy Rose Lee's sister: 'The following year, in *Sing Your Worries Away*, she played a stripper, taking off her clothes and her sister.'

CHAPTER 6

Words Are Stupid, Words Are Fun

Confused by words that look or sound alike?
How to be limpid, not limp

Words are stupid, words are fun,
Words can put you on the run.
What are words worth?
TOM TOM CLUB, 'WORDY RAPPINGHOOD'

I don't want to talk grammar. I want to talk like a
lady in a flower shop.
ELIZA DOOLITTLE, *PYGMALION*

It's easy to get words mixed up. The consequences can be comic, like Stan Laurel ordering 'moustachio' ice-cream, or potentially tragic (see 'flammable or inflammable?', below). I've spent much of my career working with words, mainly trying to unscramble the confusion and correct the mistakes before they get into print. I don't keep score, but two of the things that irritate me most are the misuse of *ironic* and *iconic*. A small consolation is that so far no one has actually mistaken one for the other, unlike the examples later in the chapter.

It Isn't Ironic

It's a black fly in your chardonnay.
It's a death row pardon two minutes too late.
And isn't it ironic … don't you think?
ALANIS MORISSETTE, 'IRONIC'

I hate to say this, Alanis, but the answer is: no. And most of the other examples in her 1995 song aren't ironic either, being variously bad luck (rain on your wedding day), bad organisation (getting stuck in a traffic jam when you're late), bad timing (meeting the man of your dreams and then discovering he has a beautiful wife), or untidiness (ten thousand spoons when all you need is a knife). Alanis is on surer ground when she turns to philosophy (life has a funny way of sneaking up on you), but she doesn't know much about irony. Which, for the composer of a song called 'Ironic', is ironic.

Not that she is alone. 'Ironic' (from the ancient Greek word *eironeia*, 'pretended ignorance') is one of the most abused words. And journalists are the worst offenders. Occasionally, the word is employed correctly: 'the humorous or mildly sarcastic use of words to imply the opposite of what they normally mean' or 'incongruity between what is expected to be and what actually is'. It seems reasonable to describe as ironic, for example, the fact that victims of flooding can be surrounded by water, but have none to drink. Or perhaps, as the comedian Ed Byrne suggested, if it rains on your wedding day when you are marrying a weatherman and he chose the date.

Too often, though, ironic is used to mean strange, mildly amusing or merely coincidental. So it is 'ironic' that an actor has been given a part in *The Lord of the Rings* films when he has not read the books (*Sunday Times*). It is 'ironic' that the boxer Ricky Hatton was knocked down by a blow to the body, as that was how he had previously knocked down many of his opponents (all papers). Sports reports are particularly susceptible to over-irony. 'Tottenham won 2–0 at Nottingham Forest,' the *Guardian* reported – 'ironic really, with the London club having a big interest in Forest's midfielder Andy Reid.' This is not so much ironic, really, as really moronic.

Kingsley Amis lamented in *The King's English*: 'The slightest and most banal coincidence or point of resemblance, or even just-perceptible absence of one, unworthy of a single grunt of interest, gets called "ironical".' Amis would have been unimpressed by 'Ironic', although Morissette has subsequently claimed that the irony of the lyrics lies in the fact that the examples she gives are not, in fact, ironic.

There's plenty of irony in pop music. In Eminem's *Stan*, it is combined with the blackest of black humour and Dido's sampled warbles to create a disturbing morality tale. But perhaps the best example of irony is when 10cc sing 'I'm not in love'. No one could doubt the ironic intent: they mean the opposite. The singer's claim that he only keeps her picture on the wall to hide a stain is fooling no one. The irony adds to the song's poignancy.

The suggested introduction of a typeface called ironics – similar to italics, but sloping the other way – has been attributed to various people, most credibly the late Labour MP Tom Driberg. Whoever it was, I assume the intention was ironic. Various attempts have been made to introduce an irony punctuation mark, perhaps a reversed question

@guardianstyle High-quality reporting; 'high quality reporting' was what Will Self did when he was covering an election campaign.

mark, to indicate irony or sarcasm. This would be the written equivalent of people who make the sign of quotation marks when they are speaking, which makes me want to give them a slap. British people sometimes say that Americans 'do not do irony', which anyone who has seen *The Simpsons* or *Curb Your Enthusiasm* knows is simply not true. Alanis Morissette, however, is Canadian.

Ironic misuse

Irritation factor: 8/10

Frequency of error: 7/10

Misused by: journalists, football commentators, Alanis Morissette

Typically annoying example:

> *Carlos Tevez struggled to score for Manchester United. So it's ironic he's just scored two against them wearing a Manchester City shirt.*
>
> (COMMENTATOR)

It Isn't Iconic, Either

> *Last week, Drake Levin of the harmless 60s pop combo Paul Revere & the Raiders passed away. Sure enough, reports immediately came in that a guitar icon from an iconic group was no longer here to be iconographic.*
>
> JOE QUEENAN

@the_itch1980 Can you clear up the bellend conundrum? 1 word, 2 words or hyphenated?

A reader wrote to me to ask: 'Which is more abused? Ironic or iconic?' Ironic, as we have seen, is in a bad way; icon and iconic, however, are in intensive care, stripped of all meaning by unthinking repetition.

A single issue of the *Guardian* I chose at random featured eight icons before breakfast: the Routemaster bus, the Lloyd's building, Blackpool, Sainsbury's, Marge Simpson, Voldemort, Shelley, and 'several iconic buildings' in Greenwich, south-east London. A day earlier, Jordan, 'a punk style icon who was a fixture at early Sex Pistols gigs', had joined Jordan, the model Katie Price, in being accorded iconic status by my newspaper.

Icon and iconic initially referred to portraits, from the Greek *eikon*, and this is what they meant as used in English from the 16th century. The words did not come to mean sacred images until the 19th century, and in the 20th century this was broadened to symbols or representatives. The first OED citation for this usage is a 1952 article about F Scott Fitzgerald's short story 'The Diamond as Big as the Ritz', 'turning a critical eye upon a national icon'.

One assumes that people who use this word so readily know what they wish to convey, but for those (like me) who no longer share their confidence, Collins dictionary gives five current definitions of icon:

- an image of Christ, the Virgin Mary or a saint venerated by the Eastern Orthodox Church;
- an image, picture or representation;
- a symbol representing or analogous to the thing it represents;

@guardianstyle Not again. Bell-end.

- a sex symbol (Jordan, perhaps, but Marge Simpson?) or symbol of a belief or cultural movement; and finally
- a symbol on a computer.

I am by no means convinced that these definitions, though wide-ranging, cover Bernard Manning's World Famous Embassy Club in Manchester; Fidel Castro's cigar; the *Countdown* TV theme; 'David Beckham wearing an anti-Glazer scarf'; 'Grace Kelly in casual wear'; grey wolves; Hove; salmon farming; the storm drains of Los Angeles; the video for Kylie's 'Can't Get You Out of My Head'; and wind turbines ('iconic renewable energy technology').

Lest you think this is just a *Guardian* thing, it's the same in all newspapers: I read the lot on a randomly selected day (28 November 2012), and discovered that the following phenomena had achieved iconic status: Bondi Beach (*Sun*, *Mirror*); blonde hair and blue eyes (*Sun*); JR Ewing (*Sun*); 'Wannabe', 'Stop', 'Spice Up Your Life' and 'Say You'll Be There' by the Spice Girls (*Sun*); Spider-Man (*Sun*); the Rolling Stones' 'Gimme Shelter' (*Mirror*); the late Jack Duckworth of *Coronation Street* (*Mirror*); *The Snowman* (*Mirror*); the *Big Brother* eye logo (*Star*); *The Wicker Man* (*Independent*); Sachin Tendulkar, 'the iconic veteran batsman' (*Independent*); the Olympic Stadium, the Aquatics Centre, the Velodrome and the Copper Box (*Telegraph*); and Tahrir Square in Cairo (*Guardian*).

Set such an example by those of us paid good money to write and edit this stuff, it is hardly surprising that iconitis has spread to those previously guilty of no worse linguistic

---

@Tom_Mullen Is 'meet with' ever acceptable?

abuses than the odd greengrocer's apostrophe, as evidenced in Asda's proud boast that its £2 chicken is – yes – 'iconic'. And iconitis can strike when you least expect it. Who could have imagined that, according to the Work Foundation, four jobs in 21st-century Britain – hairdressers, celebrities, managers and management consultants – have become 'iconic'?

A reader emailed to say: 'I suggest you reserve anything to do with icons to the Virgin Mary, Elvis Presley and a very limited number of people whose faces are recognised and revered, maybe also little figures on computer screens. Otherwise it becomes devalued and is just a trendy way of saying famous or memorable.' That man is an icon of good sense.

Iconic abuse
Irritation factor: 9/10
Frequency of error: 9/10
Misused by: journalists

Typically absurd example:

> *The cut above his eye suffered by David Beckham after being hit by a flying boot allegedly kicked by Sir Alex Ferguson was, according to the* Guardian, *'iconic'.*

@guardianstyle Maybe if you meet with triumph and disaster, but not 'meet with' someone.

More Words That Cause Confusion, Anger or Despair

> *'When I use a word,' Humpty Dumpty said in rather a scornful tone, 'it means just what I choose it to mean – neither more nor less.' 'The question is,' said Alice, 'whether you can make words mean so many different things.'*
>
> LEWIS CARROLL, *THROUGH THE LOOKING-GLASS,* AND *WHAT ALICE FOUND THERE*

> *To get the right word in the right place is a rare achievement.*
>
> MARK TWAIN

A *Guardian* report saying that the Manchester United central defenders Ferdinand and Vidić 'complimented each other' evoked a picture of Rio Ferdinand pausing during an opposition attack to say to Nemanja Vidić: 'No, you go for the ball, you look so elegant when you head it away,' and the other replying: 'Oh, you're too kind, but you really are much better in the air than I am.' The report meant to *compliment* them on the way they *complement* each other.

A homonym (from the Greek for 'having the same name') is a word with the same spelling or sound as another, but with a different meaning. A homophone is a word that sounds like another but has a different meaning or spelling, or both. So *complement* and *compliment* are both homonyms and homophones, whereas *bow* (of a ship) and *bow* (tie) are homonyms but not homophones, as they are pronounced differently. Synonyms are words with the same or similar meanings.

@ayse Why is 'rock'n'roll' one word?

Over four decades in newspapers I have seen all the following words misused at one time or another. I hope this list will help readers to avoid the same mistakes.

abstruse: hard to understand; **obtuse**: dull, stupid or insensitive.

accept: receive; **except**: exclude.
She accepted my apology and excepted me from her criticisms.

adopted children; **adoptive** parents who do the adopting.

adverse: unfavourable; **averse**: reluctant.
He was averse to crossing the Irish Sea in such adverse conditions.

advice: noun; **advise**: verb.
I'd advise you to take my advice.
The same principle applies to *device* (noun) and *devise* (verb), *prophecy* (noun) and *prophesy* (verb), in both British and American English. However, whereas in British English *licence* is a noun and *license* a verb, in American English *license* is both noun and verb. As with the others, *practice* and *practise* are respectively noun and verb in British English, but this time, to confuse us, *practice* is both noun and verb in American English.

affect (verb): have an impact on; **effect** (noun): impact.
Overwork was affecting his health but had little effect on his bank balance.
To make it interesting, *effect* is also a verb, meaning make something happen:

@guardianstyle It's a single concept (not 'rock' + 'roll') and it looks best that way.

I hope my book will effect a change in standards of reading and writing.

agenda
Plural in origin, but singular in use: *agendum* is simply not on anyone's agenda.

aggravate
> *She only wanted to threaten him and aggravate him ...*
>
> WILKIE COLLINS, *THE WOMAN IN WHITE*

Using this word to mean annoy, rather than make worse, really aggravates some people. Good. Both meanings have been around for more than 400 years, and there is no good reason why both should not be acceptable now. Note that the abbreviation of aggravation is aggro, despite the once popular football chant 'A-G, A-G-R, A-G-R-O: AGRO!'

alibi
If you have one, you were somewhere else at the time, so it's stretching the meaning to use it to just mean excuse.

all right or alright?
All right is traditionally considered more right than *alright*, which has, however, been very popular in the world of rock'n'roll ever since the Who recorded 'The Kids Are Alright' in 1965. The phrase has become a cliche, widely used in songs, films and television programmes, and wildly over-used in newspaper headlines. Kingsley Amis said 'to inscribe *alright* is gross, crass, coarse and to be avoided', though he

---

@CamillaRoseJ When writing about the government, is it meant to have a capital G?

admitted this was 'a rule without a reason'. He might have pointed to the difference between 'she got the answers all right' and 'she knew the answers, alright!'.

Similarly, note the difference between 'they were *all ready*' and 'they were *already* ready', and in 'they came in *all together*, which was *altogether* a good thing'. 'The king was in the altogether' – from an old Danny Kaye song once popular on children's radio programmes – meant the king didn't have any clothes on, but you don't hear the expression, or the song, much nowadays.

alternate: every other; **alternative**: choice.
They had to alternate by working alternate Sundays. There was no alternative.
Americans use *alternate* in both cases, which many Britons find disconcerting.

although or **though**?
Although *although* sounds better at the start of a sentence, you can use *though* in most other places, though perhaps not in formal contexts.

amend: improve; **emend**: edit.

amoral: you have no sense of right and wrong; **immoral**: you do have a sense of right and wrong, but you favour the latter.

ancestors
Ancestors precede descendants. I know this; you know this; so it is remarkable how often people get them the other way round.

@guardianstyle No. It will only encourage them.

and/or
This is horrible. Make your mind up and say either *and* or *or* – whichever is more appropriate. The same applies to the phrase *if and when*.

annex: verb; **annexe**: noun.
I'm going to annex the annexe for the afternoon.

anticipate
Purists say this should not be used to mean expect. I'm sure they have their reasons, but I can't see what's wrong with 'they did not anticipate any trouble' as this is now normal usage.

appraise: evaluate; **apprise**: inform.
After appraising his work, they apprised him that it was not up to scratch.

arcane: esoteric; **archaic**: antiquated.

ascent: climb; **assent**: agree.

assume or **presume**?
Largely interchangeable: Henry Stanley might just as easily have said 'Dr Livingstone, I assume?' these days, although you are presumed, rather than assumed, innocent.

auger (noun): used to make holes; **augur** (verb): predict.

@dollydave People who use 'myself' instead of 'me' should be shot, yes? Asking for a friend.

aural, oral or verbal?

> *Verbal does not really mean the same as oral, although it has been said that verbal sex means talking about it.*
> KEITH WATERHOUSE

Aural means to do with the ear. If you have *verbal* skills, you are good with words. All agreements are verbal, but an *oral* agreement is unwritten.

awaken

I recommend using 'I woke up', 'I was woken up', and so on, because the forms starting with A are either considered wrong ('I was awoken') or sound wrong ('I was awakened'). The American grammarian Bryan A Garner says: 'The past-tense and past-participial forms of "wake" and its various siblings are perhaps the most vexing in the language.'

bacteria

Bacteria are plural; the singular is *bacterium*. You do see bacteria used in the singular, which annoys scientists in particular, though not as much as saying bacteria when you mean *virus*. Similarly, *criteria* are plural and the singular is *criterion*.

bail out or bale out?

You *bail out* a prisoner (by standing bail for them), a company (through a *bailout*) or someone in financial difficulty (with a loan or gift).

You *bale out* a leaking boat, or from an aircraft. This is also the spelling for bale of hay and baleful expression.

@guardianstyle That's what they all say.
Tell your 'friend' we agree.

baited trap; **bated** breath.

balk or baulk?

To *balk* is to obstruct or stop short; *baulk* is an area of a snooker table.

bellwether

The sheep that leads the herd with a bell round its neck, so figuratively something that shows the way. A seat in an election might prove a *bellwether* if it points the way to the overall result.

biannual or biennial?

As no one can agree which of these means twice a year, and which means every two years, it's best not to use them at all; 'twice a year' and 'every two years' are unambiguous. The same applies to *bimonthly* and *biweekly*: say 'every fortnight', 'twice a month' or 'every two months', and so on. It's remarkable that no one has sorted this problem out; nearly a century ago, HW Fowler was already calling it 'a cause of endless confusion'.

blatant: obvious; **flagrant**: shocking.
It was a blatant foul, but banning him for 12 games was a flagrant abuse of power.

blond

An adjective, whether describing a man or a woman. Only put an E on it if you work for a tabloid newspaper and feel you need to call a woman 'a blonde'.

@CliveAndrews Who decided that 'Royal Wedding' gets capital letters? And why?

bonus

As this word already means additional, 'added bonus' is a waste of a good adjective.

born out of necessity; **borne out** by the facts.

breach of promise; **breech** birth.

brickbat

A piece of brick, 'the typical ready missile, where stones are scarce', as the OED helpfully advises. Newspapers were once very fond of contrasting brickbats with bouquets, but you don't see that so often nowadays.

brutalise

To become brutal rather than to treat brutally; for example, some prisoners were treated brutally by soldiers who had become *brutalised* by serving in Iraq. Accepting the misuse is not just lazy but causes confusion (which one is meant?) and, ultimately, means that either one meaning is lost or the word can no longer be used to mean anything.

burger: food; **burgher**: citizen.

I've seen this mistake in several newspapers, including, sadly, my own.

censor: prevent publication; **censure**: criticise severely.

You count people in a *census* (a task carried out in ancient Rome by the censors, who also did the censoring) and burn incense in a *censer*.

check

Tricky, but here goes: *check-in* and *checkout* can be used as a noun or an adjective; *check in* and *check out* are verbs. And *check out* has two meanings. So you can *check in* at the *check-in*, but if having *checked out* the *check-in* desk you prefer the *checkout* desk, by all means *check out* at the *checkout*. *Check* also has two meanings: you can *check* someone's progress by blocking their way having *checked* that they are about to catch you up. For those who disapprove of the US spelling of *check* as used (occasionally these days) instead of cash, that's how *cheque* used to be spelt in Britain.

childish or childlike?

Laughing when someone breaks wind is childish. Laughing when someone is flying a kite is childlike.

chords: musical; **cords**: vocal.

chronic

Sometimes confused with acute – short but severe – *chronic* means for a long time or constantly recurring, so chronic asthma is something you have had for years, and not a particularly bad case of it.

classic or classical?

The latter is best reserved for ancient Greece or Rome or in the phrase 'classical music'. The former is used to describe a notable example of a particular era or style.

The Goths sacked Rome in *classical* times; 'Temple of Love' by the Sisters of Mercy is a goth *classic*.

....

@nj_linguist But of course the old movie musical is Royal Wedding.

complacent: self-satisfied; **complaisant**: obliging.

complement: make complete; **compliment**: praise.

comprise, **consist**, **compose** or **constitute**?
Tricky, but to get these right, just remember that *comprise* or *consist of* mean 'made up of' while *compose* and *constitute* mean 'make up'.

So you might say a band *comprises* guitar, bass, drums and keyboards or that it *consists of* guitar, bass, drums and keyboards. You can also say the band is *composed of* those instruments. Alternatively, you could say guitar, bass, drums and keyboards *compose* or *constitute* the band.

The one thing never to say, unless you want people who know about such things to give you a look composed of, consisting of and comprising mingled pity and contempt, is 'comprised of'.

contagious or **infectious**?
A disease spread by contact, such as an STD, is *contagious*. One spread by air or water, like a cold, is *infectious*.

contemptible: deserving contempt; **contemptuous**: displaying contempt.

continual: repeatedly recurring; **continuous**: uninterrupted. *My car continually breaks down because the radiator leaks continuously.*

---

convince or **persuade**?

The former involves proof, the latter faith. Having convinced someone of the facts, you might persuade them to do something, conceivably against their better judgment.

coruscating

Perhaps misled by phrases such as 'coruscating criticism', some people confuse this with excoriating (censuring severely). In fact, *coruscating* means sparkling or emitting flashes of light, so coruscating criticism would be brilliantly written.

councillor or **counsellor**?

A *councillor* serves on a local council; a *counsellor* offers advice. A member of the *privy council* is a *privy counsellor*.

credible: believable; **credulous**: easily misled.

So *incredible* means unbelievable and *incredulous* means amazed. Don't confuse these words with *creditable*, which means deserving credit.

crescendo

Music of increasing volume, so used metaphorically should mean moving towards a climax – not the climax itself.

cum

Latin for 'with', seen in such placenames as Chorlton-cum-Hardy and such phrases as cookbook-cum-autobiography (unfortunately rendered by my own newspaper as 'cook-

....

@guardianstyle Americans need not feel left out of all the pomp and pageantry [of the royal wedding]: you do after all have Count Basie, Earl Hines, Prince & the Dukes of Hazzard ...

book-come-autobiography'). Please take my word for the accuracy of the above and under no circumstances Google to check.

cupful
The plural is cupfuls, as with spoonfuls, but it's three cups ful*l*, three spoons ful*l*.

curb: restrain; **kerb**: pavement.
Please curb your enthusiasm for driving on the kerb.

cusp
Used by many writers in phrases such as 'on the cusp of adulthood' or 'on the cusp of half-time', perhaps under the impression that 'cusp' sounds cleverer than 'brink' or 'verge'. What does sound cleverer is to use it correctly, to mean positioned between two points in time or space, as in the elegant 'poised on the cusp of classicism and romanticism'.

data
Still treated as plural in scientific and academic work, but most other people say 'the data is' rather than 'the data are'. You come across *datum*, the singular of data, about as often as you hear about an agendum.

decry: condemn; **descry**: discover.
You only ever see *descry* when someone uses it wrongly to mean *decry*.

---

definite, definitely or definitive, definitively?

For me, this is definitely the definitive grammar book.

defuse or diffuse?

The distinction seems to baffle many reporters. Luckily, subeditors have learned it at their mother's breast and usually tidy any mix-up before it gets into the paper. To *defuse* is to render harmless; to *diffuse* is to spread about.

delusion or illusion?

HW Fowler alluded to this distinction when he memorably wrote: 'That the Sun moves round the Earth was once a delusion, and is still an illusion.'

denier or sceptic?

Your choice may well reflect your politics. Some prefer to avoid *denier* as in 'global warming denier' because of connotations with Holocaust denial. Others point out that the OED definition of a *sceptic* is 'a seeker of the truth; an inquirer who has not yet arrived at definite conclusions', which is highly flattering to 'climate change sceptics' who are literally in denial about the evidence – 'they will believe any old rubbish that suits their cause' is how one member of the *Guardian*'s environment team puts it. In a similar vein, you might argue that Europhobic would be more accurate than Eurosceptic. There's no right or wrong answer, except to say that if you type 'denier' into Google, it will probably direct you to a site selling hosiery as it is a weight of fibre. Oh, and 'denialist' is not a word.

@midnightcourt The queen this, the royal that. You are not the boss of English! : p

dependant: noun; **dependent**: adjective.
His dependants were dependent on him for everything.

deprecate: express disapproval; **depreciate**: fall in value.
Hence *self-deprecating* humour, remark, and so on.

derisive or **derisory**?
The former means contemptuous, as in a yell of *derision*; the latter means unworthy of serious discussion, as in a *derisory* offer.

dilemma
Not just a posh word for decision. It suggests a choice between two difficult courses of action: you could face a *dilemma*, for example, about whether to call Republican party members in the US climate change deniers or sceptics. The best known example of a dilemma in literature is 'to be or not to be'.

disassemble: take apart; **dissemble**: conceal.

disburse: give out money; **disperse**: scatter a crowd.
If you are not sure about these two, neither is Dan Brown: he got it wrong in *The Da Vinci Code*.

discomfit or **discomfort**?
The meaning between these two is so blurred as to be in effect meaningless. The first is meant to carry a sense of embarrassment and the second a lack of comfort. So let's all agree to say things like 'the minister was *discomfited* by Paxman's questions and looked increasingly uncomfortable as the interview continued'.

discreet: circumspect; **discrete**: unrelated.

Lonely hearts ads placed by attached people looking for a bit on the side sometimes say they are seeking 'a *discrete* relationship'. (Or so I am told.) They mean *discreet*.

disinterested or uninterested?

Disinterested is the negative form of interested as in 'interested party', so it means unbiased. *Uninterested* is the negative form of interested as in 'interested in football', so it means not taking an interest. This seems perfectly straightforward, and those of us who were taught it get understandably upset when some oik comes along who wasn't. True, disinterested did mean uninterested into the 17th century – John Donne, for example, used it in this sense – and a lot of people have started doing so again. They are defended by the provisional wing of the descriptivists on the grounds of language change, though presumably not on the grounds that they think it's helpful for disinterested and uninterested to be used to mean *the same thing*.

distinct or distinctive?

There's a distinct possibility that he will insist on showing you the distinctive birthmark on his left buttock.

douse: soak; **dowse**: search for water.

due to or owing to?

Getting these the wrong way round upsets a lot of people. Announcements such as 'the train is late due to leaves on the line' sound wrong to me because I was taught the following:

@KevinJBall But shouldn't Prince have a capital, as it is a title?

if you can substitute 'caused by' or 'the result of', *due to* is correct; if you can substitute 'because of', *owing to* is correct.

So my suggestion is to avoid *due to* and *owing to* altogether and say:

- The train's late arrival was caused by the wrong kind of snow.
- The train was late because of the wrong kind of snow.

You can also say 'because' instead of 'due to the fact that' or 'owing to the fact that', and save a lot of space, as well as aggravation.

Of course, 'due to' has another meaning – we are due to arrive in 10 minutes – which everyone understands and no one argues about.

each other or one another?

Purists say the former should apply only to two people ('Iniesta and Xavi hugged each other') and the latter to more than two ('all 11 Spanish players hugged one another'). HW Fowler was unimpressed by this argument and in my experience very few people make the distinction, especially during an exciting football match.

effectively

This adverb is best kept simply to describe how something was done: 'Anna managed the department *effectively*.' Confusion arises when it is used instead of 'in effect', which describes something that has the effect of, even if the effect was unintended or unofficial: 'Her boss was off, so in effect Anna was the manager of the department' is clearer than it would be if 'in effect' was replaced by 'effectively'. Some writers use effectively in neither of these ways, but just to pad out a sentence in a feeble attempt at adding emphasis, in which case I always delete it.

effete

The traditional meaning is spent or worn out, but nowadays you rarely see this word used to mean anything other than effeminate or foppish. Baroness Orczy used it in this sense in *The Scarlet Pimpernel* as long ago as 1905: 'Those happy days of courtship, before he had become the lazy nincompoop, the effete fop, whose life seemed spent in card and supper rooms.'

eke out

This used to mean making a small amount go further, as in 'she eked out her rations by serving string instead of spaghetti'. It was a bit extra – note that *eke* meant 'also' as used by Chaucer. The word has come to mean something rather different, namely scraping by, as in 'she eked out a living doing the occasional subbing shift at the *Sunday Times*'. Now, can we all agree that this is an example of language change that no one can seriously object to?

elegy: poem of mourning; **eulogy**: speech of praise.
The adjective *elegiac*, sometimes misspelt 'elegaic', is very popular with writers on upmarket newspapers seeking an alternative to *sad*.

elemental: basic; **elementary**: simple.

@Daveip1966 But obviously Queen refers to Freddie, Brian, John & Roger.

emigrate: leave a country; **immigrate**: arrive in one.
Hence *emigrant* and *immigrant*. A *migrant* does either. An 'economic migrant' is how rightwing newspapers and politicians describe someone who immigrates to the UK to do what emigrants from the UK do when they move to other countries.

eminent: distinguished; **imminent**: about to happen.
I dimly recall Peter Lorre's character, Joel Cairo, getting these two mixed up in *The Maltese Falcon*, or perhaps in a parody of that fine film noir.

emotional: showing emotion; **emotive**: causing emotion.
Badger culling is an *emotive* issue. No wonder people get *emotional* about it.
Tired and emotional is a euphemism for drunk.

emulate or **imitate**?
The traditional meaning of *emulate* is to attempt to equal or surpass, so 'try to emulate' is strictly tautologous. But nowadays if you say 'he emulated Thatcher', everyone will think you mean that he succeeded, so you do need to qualify it. To *imitate* might involve a handbag and the phrase 'the lady is not for turning'.
He sought to emulate Thatcher, but ended up doing a poor imitation of Major.

enormity
It might sound a bit like 'enormous', but *enormity* refers to something monstrous or wicked, such as a massacre, not big.

@guardianstyle Precisely: 'the Queen' = Elizabeth II, 'Queen' = band.

ensure: make certain; **insure**: protect against risk.
But just to keep you on your toes, you can also *assure* someone's life by buying an insurance policy.

epicentre
An *epicentre* is the place on the Earth's surface above the point of origin of an earthquake. It is not a posh word for centre, although widely used to mean that by people who think it somehow sounds more authoritative.

equable: even; **equitable**: fair.
His temperament, like the climate, was equable. None the less, he demanded a more equitable share of the proceeds.

ere or **e'er**?
It's *ere* long (soon) and *ere* now (before); *e'er*, which you might come across in an old poem, is an abbreviation of ever.

erupt: burst out; **irrupt**: burst in.

especially or **specially**?
The former means particularly ('he was *especially* fond of crab') or in particular ('this policy is aimed at Ukip voters, *especially* those in marginal seats'). The latter means for a special reason ('she made crab sandwiches *specially* for him'). If a company claims a product has been designed 'especially for you', it hasn't.

everyday: ordinary; **every day**: daily.
Drinking was an everyday event; they went to the pub every day.

@BeatriceJBray What would CP Scott think of the absence of a cap G in @guardianstyle?

exalt: praise someone; **exult**: rejoice.
Tony Blair was exalted as exultant New Labour supporters exulted.

exceptional: above average; **exceptionable**: something you take exception to.
The roast beef was exceptional, but the yorkshire pudding was exceptionable.

exhausting: tiring; **exhaustive**: thorough.

expatriate
I often see this word misspelt as ex-pat, ex-patriate or ex-patriot. But this is 'ex' meaning out of (as in export or extract), not 'ex-' meaning former (as in ex-husband). Those who can't spell it should consider using 'immigrant', a term less redolent of the days of empire and one that they are happy enough to apply to people from other countries.

farther, **farthest** or **further**, **furthest**?
Because of their similarity to 'far', it makes sense to use the former pair when relating to distance: 'a few miles *farther*, and we will reach the *farthest* point'. *Further* and *furthest* are much more versatile: you can use them for distance as well as anything to do with matters of degree. I will go further, and further the argument that you have to use *further* in certain cases, for example when asking for further details, so let's not consider this subject any further.

@guardianstyle He was very progressive. We think he'd understand.

fatal: deadly; **fateful**: momentous.
The fateful game arrived. It was to prove fatal for Wednesday's chances of promotion.

fayre
A fete worse than death.

faze: overwhelm; **phase**: stage.
Everything seemed to faze him but it turned out to be just a phase.

ferment or **foment**?
You *foment* unrest, but *ferment* alcohol.

few: some but not many; **a few**: not many but some.
Few grammarians make good teachers, but a few do.

flammable or **inflammable**?
'Why do flammable and inflammable mean the same thing?' asked Rob Lowe's character in *The West Wing*. You can see why: *flammable* is in flames; *inflammable* inflames. This could be quite dangerous in, say, a firefighting situation ('It's OK, guys – it says it's INflammable … oops!'). To avoid confusion, for the opposite of *flammable* use *non-flammable*.

flaunt or **flout**?
Think of Max Bialystock in the funniest film ever made – *The Producers* – admiring a white Rolls-Royce in the street: 'That's it, baby, when you've got it, flaunt it, flaunt it!' Then think of Bialystock and Bloom, his partner, flouting the law – as

---

@Andrew_Taylor What's the basis for not capitalising 'mecca' or 'machiavellian'?

well as the principles of good taste – by staging *Springtime for Hitler*.

flotsam and **jetsam**
The former is cargo or wreckage found floating in the sea; the latter (originally a variant of *jettison*) is stuff that has been thrown overboard. Used together to mean odds and ends.

forbear (verb): hold back; **forebear** (noun): ancestor.
I forbear from blaming my forebears for my family's lack of ambition.

forensic
This is not a synonym for scientific. It means relating to courts of law – so all evidence in court is *forensic*, a forensic scientist is one whose work is used for legal purposes, and forensic medicine means medical jurisprudence. Newspapers sometimes call scientific evidence 'forensic evidence'.

forever: continually; **for ever**: for always.
She is forever changing her mind, but I shall love her for ever.

forgo: go without; **forego**: go before.
You don't want to know this, but I'm going to tell you anyway: the past tense of *forgo* is *forwent*, and the past participle *forgone*; the past tense of *forego* is *forewent*, and the past participle *foregone*, as in 'foregone conclusion'.

formally: in a formal manner; **formerly**: in the past.
Everyone knows this, but they are frequently mixed up.
He formerly dressed formally, but now he's a slob.

***

@guardianstyle A weakening of the connections to Machiavelli or Mecca.

fortuitous: accidental; **fortunate**: lucky.

The same football commentators who ruled that deflections must always be described as 'wicked' also decided that fortunate or lucky does not sound as impressive as *fortuitous*. They do not, however, mean the same thing.

founder: fail; **flounder**: flail.

A business will typically *founder* (think of a sinking ship) because its managers *flounder* (think of a drowning man).

fulsome

Not a fancy word for full, it indicates lavish excess, as in 'fulsome praise' or this eloquent description in the *London Review of Books*, by Rosemary Hill, of books about the Queen Mother: 'His biography was pious to a degree and, like his equally fulsome edition of her letters, much too long.'

geriatrics

A branch of medicine. Also occasionally used by younger people to describe older people, perhaps intended to be humorous. It won't seem so funny when they're old.

grill: on an oven; **grille**: on a car or a gate.

grisly: gruesome; **grizzly**: grey.

hail fellow, well met; **hale** and hearty.

heave

There is confusion about the past tense, which is *heaved* in the senses of 'she heaved a sigh of relief as he heaved the knife

---

away', but *hove* in other senses: 'They hove into view, hove up the anchor and hove alongside.' In all the above cases, the present tense is *heave* or *heaves*, so it would be 'they heave into view'.

historic or historical?
A *historic* event is notable, a *historical* event merely something that happened in the past. While we are at it, 'an historic' is considered old-fashioned and in modern English 'a historic', 'a hotel', and so on, sound more natural. Before silent H, the opposite applies: 'an heir', 'an honest man', and so on.

hoard or horde?
A *hoard* of treasure; a *horde* (or hordes) of tourists. Often confused.

home in on
Not 'hone in on', which points to a need to hone one's writing skills.

homogeneous or homogenous?
The latter, a biological term meaning having common descent, is often misused for the former, which means of the same kind.

humerus: bone; humorous: funny.
The 'funny bone' is the ulnar nerve, which like the humerus is in your arm. Hence, the not very humorous old joke: 'Getting hit in the funny bone is not humerus.'

imply: suggest; **infer**: conclude.

> *Homer: What are you inferring?*
> *Lisa: I'm not inferring anything. You infer; I imply.*
> *Homer: Well that's a relief.*
> THE SIMPSONS

No one uses *imply* to mean *infer*, but many people use *infer* when they mean *imply*. If you do so, you are in good company: Milton, Sir Walter Scott and Mervyn Peake in *Titus Groan* all did it.

impractical or **impracticable**?
After much study, I have come to the conclusion that these words mean the same thing. And as reference books typically define the former as 'not practical', and the latter as 'not able to be done', who is going to disagree with me?

inchoate
Nothing to do with chaos, it means newly formed, whether describing someone's literary skills or the universe shortly after the big bang.

insidious: gradually harmful; **invidious**: likely to arouse resentment.
A disease can be *insidious*; a person can be put in an *invidious* position. Even though this distinction is in my own style guide, I have to look it up every time.

intense: extreme; **intensive**: thorough.
The search, which aroused *intense* opposition from local people, was *intensive*.

@JaymeDetweiler #APStyle fun fact, it is government shutdown not government shut down

interned: imprisoned; **interred**: buried.

interpreter
Works with the spoken word; often confused with *translator*, who works with the written word.

into or **in to**?
If you go *into* a room or look *into* something, it's one word; if you call *in to* complain, listen *in to* someone's conversation or go *in to* see them, it's two. *On to* is two words, although Kingsley Amis slightly overdid it when he declared: 'I have found by experience that no one persistently using *onto* writes anything much worth reading.'

inveigh: attack; **inveigle**: coax.
Labour MPs might have *inveighed* against Tony Blair for *inveigling* them into the plan to invade Iraq.

jejune
Naive or unsophisticated, not necessarily anything to do with youth. Although *jeune* means young in French, *jejune* is derived from the Latin for fasting and originally meant deficient or scanty. The OED's first listing of it in the modern sense is from George Bernard Shaw's *Arms and the Man*, published in 1898.

knell or **knoll**?
A *knell* is the sound of a bell, hence 'death knell'. A bell can be knelled, as well as tolled. A *knoll* is a small hill, not necessarily grassy.

@guardianstyle 'Fun fact'?

larva: insect; **lava**: volcanic magma, lamp.
And *larverbread*, not 'lavabread', is cooked seaweed.

latter
Saying an item is 'the latter' of more than two things is not only annoying but also wrong. In such cases, it should be 'last'. It's best to treat *latter* as I have done in this chapter, and use it only in contrast with *former*.

led or lead?
In all but the present tense, the verb form is *led*. This does not stop otherwise normal, sensible people writing things like 'he was lead to the slaughter' or 'the singing will be lead by Cliff Richard'. If this is just a slip of the keyboard, it's a frequent slip.

licence or license?
In British English, licence is the noun and license the verb. So you need a *licence* to run a *licensed* bar, or you may need to visit the *off-licence*.

lightening or lightning?
Your hair may be *lightening* in colour, but that electrical stuff in the sky is *lightning*.

likely
In the UK, if not the US, using *likely* in such contexts as 'they will likely win the game' sounds unnatural at best; there is no good reason to use it instead of *probably*. If you really must do so, however, just put *very*, *quite* or *most* in front of it and all will, very likely, be well.

@zoelouwhite 'Ladies that lunch' or 'Ladies who lunch'? (Please say who...)

limp: drooping; **limpid**: clear.

loathe: detest; **loth**: reluctant.
I'm loth to do anything he says because I loathe him so much.
You sometimes see *loth* spelt as *loath*, which is not incorrect,
but only adds to the confusion with *loathe*.

luxuriant: lush; **luxurious**: expensive.
*He had his luxuriant moustache waxed at the most luxurious
salon in Bootle.*

majority
Unless you are specifically talking about the larger part of a
measurable number, *most of* normally sounds more natural.
*A clear majority had voted Conservative, so he resolved to spend
most of the next five years in the pub.*

manner or **manor**?
'To the manner born' is a phrase from Hamlet. *To the Manor
Born* was a sitcom.

masterful or **masterly**?
The former (often misused to mean the latter) means wilful
or domineering; the latter means highly competent.
He gave a masterly demonstration of good grammar.

mean or **median**?
To calculate the *mean*, commonly known as the average, you
add up everyone's wages (for example) and divide them by
the number of wage earners. The *median* is the wage earned

---

by the middle person when everyone's wages are lined up from the smallest to the largest. The median is often a more useful guide than the mean, which can be distorted by figures at one extreme or the other.

media
The media, including social media, are plural, so television might be your favourite *medium* of all the *media*. A convention of spiritualists, however, would be attended by *mediums*.

meretricious or meritorious?
Derived from the Latin for prostitute, *meretricious* – a word applied to me by a colleague on my very first night at the *Guardian* – means flashy but without substance, unlike *meritorious*, which means worthy of merit. Perhaps he meant that.

militate or mitigate?
To militate against is to influence something; to mitigate means to make less severe.
Her record militated against her early release, but in mitigation her counsel argued that she came from a broken home.

misanthropist: hates everyone; misogynist: hates women.

mutual
Simon Heffer and other sticklers say *mutual* should only mean reciprocated – mutual respect, mutual admiration society, mutual destruction – rather than shared. By this logic, Dickens would have had to change the title of *Our Mutual Friend* to *Our Common Friend*.

@CylonCymon 'We'll send that over to yourselves to sign' #argh

myriad

A large, unspecified number, derived from the ancient Greek for ten thousand. The OED lists various ways it is used: as a singular noun (there is *a myriad* of people outside), a plural noun (there are *myriads* of people outside), or an adjective (there are *myriad* people outside).

naught: nothing; **nought**: the figure 0.

negligent: careless; **negligible**: slight.

noisome

Nothing to do with noise, it means offensive or evil-smelling. Looking at what has happened to *fulsome*, it seems likely that lazy people will start using *noisome* as a fancy way to mean noisy, which would be a shame.

ongoing

Bureaucrats and business people love this jargon word and even some journalists are oddly fond of it, although the story has yet to be written that cannot be improved by removing it. 'Ongoing situation' or 'on an ongoing basis' are even worse.

over

Already an adverb, so 'overly' is unnecessary. The same applies to 'regardlessly', regardless of how you feel about it, and 'irregardless' is not a word at all. Similar examples include last, not 'lastly', and least, not 'leastly'.

@guardianstyle Agreed. They should be humanely destroyed.

palate, palette or pallet?

The *palate* is the roof of the mouth or sense of taste; an artist mixes paint on a *palette*; a *pallet* is one of those wooden frames you see on a forklift truck.

pale

The expression 'beyond the pale', meaning unacceptable, outside the boundary, has nothing to do with buckets; it is derived from the Latin *palus*, a stake used to support a fence, from which *palisade* is also derived.

partakes

If you must, it is *partakes of*, not 'partakes in', but it sounds pompous and quaint.

partly or partially?

Use *partial* or *partially* only to mean the opposite of impartial, except in the phrase 'partial eclipse'; otherwise *partly*.
I may be being partial, but booking me to stay in a partly built hotel merits a refund.

patronise

To *patronise* is to be snobbish about someone or something. For example, many grammar books adopt a patronising attitude towards their readers, branding their mistakes 'illiterate'. If you use it to mean shop somewhere ('I patronise my local Budgens'), you will sound like a twerp.

pedal a bike; peddle drugs.

@MrsVauvenargues Would it be a great-aunt or a grand-aunt?

peremptory: not open to challenge; **perfunctory**: careless.
If you carry out a task in a *perfunctory* way, you may face *peremptory* dismissal.

perspicacious: shrewd; **perspicuous**: easily understood.
But only if you are showing off.

peruse
Some maintain that to *peruse* is to scrutinise or study carefully, rather than browse or skim, although Samuel Johnson defined it in the latter sense. So if you use it, your meaning will be unclear and, even if you are being ironic, you will sound pretentious.

picaresque or **picturesque**?
A *picaresque* novel is one in which the hero is a rogue who has a series of adventures – for example, Henry Fielding's *The Adventures of Tom Jones, a Foundling* (1749) or John Kennedy Toole's *A Confederacy of Dunces* (1980). Nothing to do with *picturesque*, visually pleasing.

pleasantry
A playful word or joke, not just something pleasant.

popular: liked; **populist**: wants to be liked.
The party's policies may have been populist, but its politicians remained unpopular.

pore or **pour**?
You might *pore* over this book having *poured* out a cup of coffee. You would be amazed how often journalists (and, I presume, other people) get these mixed up.

precede: go before; **proceed**: go ahead.

precipitate: sudden; **precipitous**: steep.

prescribe, prescriptive: do something; **proscribe, proscriptive**: don't.
Prescriptive grammarians love to tell you what to do and to proscribe things they disapprove of.

presently
What exactly does this mean? I will tell you *presently* – soon – is the traditional British English usage, whereas in American English it means at present, and is usually redundant ('we are presently third in the table'). To avoid ambiguity, say *soon* when you mean soon, and don't say anything when you mean now. There is a similar problem with *momentarily*, which means 'for a moment' or 'briefly' in British English, and 'very soon' to American (and some British) speakers. To be clear, avoid.

prestigious
For centuries this meant deceptive, as in a conjuring trick (*prestidigitation*). When I trained as a journalist in the 1970s, we were told never to use it to mean conferring prestige or status. We ignored this advice, as most people were using it in precisely that way, and now everyone does.

@CliveAndrews South America or Latin America?

prevaricate or **procrastinate**?
The former, which means speaking or acting with intent to deceive, is often confused with the latter, which means putting something off. Those contemplating the use of *prevaricate* should consider whether *equivocate* (using ambiguous language to avoid speaking directly) or *vacillate* (being indecisive) may be closer to the meaning they wish to convey.

principal: first in importance; **principle**: standard of conduct.
A vital principle, perhaps my principal rule in life, is to always split the infinitive.

pristine
If you restore something to *pristine* splendour, you have returned it to its original state, not just given it a bit of a clean.

prodigal
Wasteful or extravagant: the prodigal son may have wandered off, but he was *prodigal* because he wasted his inheritance. Thus a prodigal striker is one who misses lots of chances to score goals, not one who has played for lots of clubs (who will invariably be described as 'much-travelled').

profession
Strictly, to enter a profession you need a specific qualification, such as that acquired by a doctor, lawyer, social worker or teacher. As anyone with a mobile, a laptop and a bit of cheek can be a journalist, or at least claim to be one, journalism is not a profession but a trade, craft or racket. Much the same applies to politics.

@guardianstyle They are different.
Latin America, for example, includes Mexico.

program or **programme**?
The former is the American English version of the latter. However, it is used everywhere in relation to computing so even British people might watch a television *programme* about a new computer *program*.

prone or **supine**?
The former means face down, the latter face up.

protagonist
The person who drives the action, from the ancient Greek meaning 'first actor'. Not the same as adversary or rival, so strictly you can't have 'two protagonists'.

purposely: on purpose; **purposefully**: with determination.

pyrrhic
A *pyrrhic* victory is not a hollow one, as often assumed, but one achieved at great cost. King Pyrrhus of Epirus defeated the Romans twice, in 280BC and 279BC, but suffered such heavy losses that he said one more such victory would undo him.

quite
'I'm *quite* tired' means 'I'm fairly tired'.

'Have you *quite* finished?' means 'Have you completely finished?', and comes with a built-in note of irritation.

'*Quite!*' means 'I agree!'

This is a word that you can use in all innocence in an email only to discover later that you have offended the recipient, so

---

@usacycling Can 'rule book' ever be written as one word? #APStyle it might be better to say *completely*, *fairly* or something else less prone to ambiguity.

rack or **wrack**?
You *rack* your brains, face *rack* and ruin, and are *racked* with guilt, shame or pain. Meanwhile, *wrack* is seaweed.

radiographer: takes x-rays; **radiologist**: reads them.

ravage or **ravish**?
To *ravage* is to destroy or severely damage something. To *ravish*, confusingly, can mean one of two distinct things: to seize someone and carry them off, or to enrapture. The OED gives examples, both from the 1990s, of a child being ravished by a lion and a wine lover being ravished by a glass of chablis.

rebut, **refute** or **repudiate**?
To *rebut* is to contest or deny something; to *refute* is to prove that it's wrong. So when a politician claims to have refuted an allegation, what they mean is rebut. To *repudiate* someone is to disown them. If you don't know the difference, you could always try 'refudiate', a word coined by Sarah Palin, perhaps inspired by George W Bush's 'misunderestimate'.

recourse, resource or **resort**?
You might have *recourse* to your mother to comfort you when your hamster dies. She would, therefore, be a *resource* you could turn to. As a last *resort*, you might *resort* to your brother as well.

@guardianstyle Yes! Just miss out space between 'rule' and 'book'.

regrettably: unfortunately; **regretfully**: with regret.
Regrettably, I am unable to attend, she told him regretfully.

reign or rein?

A ruler *reigns*, but a horse is *reined in*.

respective

Unnecessary in a sentence like 'Smith and Jones spoke on behalf of their respective constituencies'; essential in 'Smith and Jones represented the constituents of Dorset North and Dorset South respectively'.

rifle: ransack, pillage; riffle: flip through a book or magazine.

round or around?

I was trying to find my way *round* the town: I was sightseeing.
I was trying to find my way *around* the town: I was looking for the ring road.

sanction

An odd word in that it can mean permit or forbid. To *sanction* (verb) something is to approve it. To impose *sanctions* (noun) is to try to stop something you disapprove of.

scotch

Scottish (not 'Scotch') people, also known as Scots, make scotch whisky, usually known simply as *scotch*. Other countries, including Canada and Japan, also make whisky. In Ireland and the United States – countries that you will note

---

@stillawake Is 'pressurising' acceptable?
It sounds awful to me

have an E in their name – they make whiskey with an E. You can also *scotch* (put an end to) someone's hopes or plans.

sea change or **step-change**?
Used interchangeably, typically to mean nothing more than 'a big change', but there is a difference that you might think worth preserving. Shakespeare coined the former in a well-known passage of *The Tempest*:

> *Full fathom five thy father lies;*
> *Of his bones are coral made;*
> *Those are pearls that were his eyes;*
> *Nothing of him that doth fade,*
> *But doth suffer a sea change,*
> *Into something rich and strange.*

The idea is that a major transformation is taking place, but very slowly. By contrast, *step-change* comes from physics, where it means an abrupt change in a value, as in voltage.

shall or **will**?
This used to be regarded as a very important distinction and some people still get excited about it. I should like to know why; I would like to know very much. Because there is very little difference these days. Use the former for emphasis ('you *shall* go to the ball'), and don't worry too much. They seem to get by quite happily in the US hardly bothering with 'shall' at all.

slither: slide; **sliver**: small piece.
Writers often get this wrong, saying things like 'a tiny *slither* of the global population' when they mean *sliver*.

@guardianstyle It sounds awful to us too.
Say put pressure on or press.

stationary: motionless; **stationery**: stuff you buy in Ryman.

straight or **strait**?

The adjective is normally *straight*, whether to describe a road or a person. It's *strait* in 'straitjacket' or 'strait-laced', 'strait-ened circumstances', placenames such as 'the strait of Dover' or 'the strait of Gibraltar', and the rock band Dire Straits.

substitute

Is it *by*, *with* or *for*? If you don't choose the right preposition, it's not always easy to see who's replaced whom.

Let's say Wayne Rooney is injured and Ryan Giggs comes on as a substitute. So: Sir Alex replaces Rooney *with* Giggs; Rooney is replaced *by* Giggs; Ferguson has substituted Giggs *for* Rooney; Giggs is substituted *for* Rooney.

till

Not an abbreviation of until; till is actually the older word. *Until* sounds more natural as the first word of a sentence and before a verb ('Until you come back to me'); *till* works well in less formal contexts and before a noun ('till lunchtime'). Do not use til or 'til, despite such precedents as the Beach Boys' sublime ''Til I Die'.

titillate: mildly excite; **titivate**: tidy up.

I recommend 'tidy up' rather than *titivate* because people will probably think you mean *titillate* and, even if they don't, they will think you sound like Ken Dodd.

@tristansmells Funner or more fun? In middle of an intense grammar debate!

torpid, **turbid** or **turgid**?
There's plenty of opportunity to get these wrong, and plenty of people do: *torpid* means apathetic or sluggish; *turbid* is muddy, thick or cloudy; *turgid* means congested or swollen, and therefore can be handy if you want to accuse someone of using bombastic or pompous language.

tortuous or **torturous**?
A long and winding road is *tortuous*. An experience involving pain or suffering might be described as *torturous*.

transpire
To emit vapour through the skin, so by analogy to become apparent, come to be known, not just a synonym for 'occur' or 'happen'; 'it transpired that' usually sounds artificial and pompous in any case.

triumphal or **triumphant**?
You might put up a *triumphal* arch because you are *triumphant*.

venal: open to bribery; **venial**: easily forgiven.
A very common, but legally dangerous, mistake.

veracity: honesty; **voracious**: having a large appetite.

waiver or **waver**?
To *waive* is to relinquish a claim or right, as in the much used headline 'Britannia waives the rules'. The associated noun is *waiver*, which can lead to confusion with *waver*, meaning to

hesitate. Adding to the fun, waver is sometimes mixed up with *haver*, which in Scotland means to talk nonsense.

weave

One word with two meanings and different past tenses. The past tense is *wove* and the past participle *woven* if you are weaving fabric, even metaphorically, as in 'Obama's speech was woven throughout with the language of the US constitution'. If you are weaving from side to side, the past tense is *weaved*, as in 'Cameron dodged and weaved'.

zhoosh

An example of polari (gay slang) used in the fashion industry and on US television shows such as *Will and Grace* and *Queer Eye for the Straight Guy*, listed here because the first time it appeared in the *Guardian* it took us several days to agree on how to spell it (this was before it had found its way into dictionaries). It can be used as a verb ('zhoosh yourself up'), a noun meaning ornamentation, or an adjective (zhooshy) meaning showy. The first example listed in the OED, which sounds like Julian and Sandy in the old BBC radio comedy *Round the Horne*, is this from 1977: 'As feely homies ... we would zhoosh our riahs, powder our eeks, climb into our bona new drag, don our batts and troll off to some bona bijou bar.'

CHAPTER 7

Pretentious, Moi?

If you are going to embroider your English with
foreign words, get them right

> *Some farre journeyed gentlemen at their returne home,*
> *like as they loue to goe in forraine apparell, so thei*
> *will pouder their talke with ouersea language. He that*
> *cometh lately out of Fraunce, will talke French English*
> *and never blush at the matter.*
>
> THOMAS WILSON, 1553

> *Homosexuality? What barbarity! It's half Greek and*
> *half Latin!*
>
> TOM STOPPARD, *THE INVENTION OF LOVE*

Wilson, the scholar quoted above, was involved in the 'inkhorn
controversy' of the 16th century in which some people argued
that too many foreign words, and in particular those from
ancient Greece and Rome, were being adopted into English.
The term comes from the suggestion that a lot of extra ink
would be needed to write them all down as they were unnecessarily long. Some words were made to resemble Latin by
the addition of superfluous extra letters, such as the B in *debt*.
Hence Mercutio's attack on 'the immortal passado, the punto
reverso' of Tybalt in *Romeo and Juliet*: 'The pox of such antic,
lisping, affecting fantasticoes; these new tuners of accents! ...

these fashion-mongers, these *pardonnez-mois*, who stand so much on the new form that they cannot sit at ease on the old bench? Oh, their *bons*, their *bons!*' In due course things settled down and no one disputes that the richness of English vocabulary owes everything to words it has acquired from elsewhere.

However, you need to be careful when using foreign and foreign-derived words in English conversation in order to avoid becoming what John Dryden described as one of 'those Fopps, who value themselves on their Travelling, and pretend they cannot express their meaning in English, because they would put off to us some French phrase of the last Edition'. A *bon vivant*, for example, appreciates good food and wine and is the correct expression to use, if you must, rather than *bon viveur*, which is a rather old-fashioned way of describing a man about town or pleasure seeker. (Think Nigel Farage, or Leslie Phillips in a black-and-white film saying 'Well helloo … ') Like *nom de plume* and *la plume de ma tante est sur le bureau de mon oncle*, actual French people do not use this phrase, although they do use *bon vivant* to mean jovial. A *gourmet*, like a bon vivant, has refined taste in food and drink. A *gourmand* is a glutton. Despite this, people often use it to mean gourmet, and sometimes get away with it.

What all these expressions have in common is that if you use them you will sound as if you are trying to show off or as if you think they are funny in an ironic kind of way, which is just as bad – one reason I didn't call Alanis Morissette 'the Canadian chanteuse' in chapter 6. I might have called myself a *soi-disant* grammar nerd, which is also pretentious, although at least I would have been using it correctly to mean self-styled (it's increasingly used to mean so-called).

@nlewendon Super injunction or superinjunction?

If you use foreign words, get them right. The two Us in *de rigueur* are de rigueur, and if you keep spelling it 'de rigeur', maybe you should try *obligatory* instead. I reintroduced Spanish accents to the *Guardian* – they had been dropped a few years earlier as everyone kept getting them wrong – after receiving the following letter from a reader: 'You wrote a short note on the meaning of the Spanish film title *Y tu Mamá También*. I hope you can read the accents I have put on the words *mamá* and *también*. If you don't place them there, you will be saying, instead of "and your mother too", something like "and you suck it too".' Similarly, without the tilde 'Happy new year' (*Feliz año nuevo*) became 'Happy new anus' (*Feliz ano nuevo*).

Despite such warnings, some people love foreign accents, whether authentic or not. Where does Häagen-Dazs ice-cream come from? The Bronx in New York City, that's where. The name, including the umlaut, was made up to give a European cachet to the product. In music, the heavier the band, the more likely that an umlaut is likely to appear in their name, which rarely affects the pronunciation but looks quite good on the T-shirt: Mötley Crüe, Motörhead and many others. As David St Hubbins of Spinal Tap observed: 'It's like a pair of eyes. You're looking at the umlaut, and it's looking at you.' Although not when your computer refuses to accept an umlaut on an N.

The blogger Alex Wain has identified foreign words for which there is no equivalent in English, including:

- *age-otori* (Japanese): to look worse after a haircut;
- *gigil* (Filipino): the urge to pinch or squeeze something cute;

- *ilunga* (Tshiluba, Congo): a person who is ready to forgive any abuse for the first time, to tolerate it a second time, but never a third time;
- *sgriob* (Gaelic): the itchiness that affects the upper lip just before taking a sip of whisky; and
- *Waldeinsamkeit* (German): the feeling of being alone in the woods.

However do we manage?

If you attempt to write in a foreign language in which you are not fluent, the effect may be something like this Indonesian news report:

> *A herd of wild elephants coming in tens of them, have been obtruding Balairaja subdistrict in Riau since weekend, and the number increased to more than forty as of Monday.*
>
> *The elephants' rush caused local residents to remain nervous and uneasy for those wild animals, honking their trunks while intruding into the village, have damaged four resident houses, eaten plants at the community gardens and undoubtedly scared of the people around.*
>
> *'I saw them with my naked eyes, at least there were forty of these mammals with long prehensile trunks really vandalizing our civilization,' a Balairaja residents muttered.*
>
> *Another villager whose house was completely smashed by a mass invasion of these four-legged jumbos with tusks claimed that his family were already evacuated.*

@Smart_Translate Does this get the prize for the most unusual word ? Cuckquean (a female cuckold)

> *'Look at my house! It's gone. These animals have*
> *eaten anything including my house,' he angered. 'Awhile*
> *ago, two big elephants collapsed my house, and they*
> *just disappeared behind the bush and came back to*
> *gluttonously eat the major of rice fields in the subdistrict,'*
> *Simbolon raised his voice raggedly.*

I'm not making fun of people taking a brave stab at what to them is a second or even third language. Their English is much better than my Indonesian. And I've got a horrible idea that this may be what my A-level French sounds like to a French person.

It's All Latin to Me

> *Away with him! Away with him! He speaks Latin.*
> SHAKESPEARE, *HENRY VI PART 2*

> *Let schoolmasters puzzle their brain,*
> *With grammar, and nonsense, and learning;*
> *Good liquor, I stoutly maintain,*
> *Gives 'genus' a better discerning.*
> *Let them brag of their heathenish gods,*
> *Their Lethes, their Styxes, and Stygians,*
> *Their 'quis', and their 'quaes', and their 'quods',*
> *They're all but a parcel of pigeons.*
> OLIVER GOLDSMITH, *SHE STOOPS TO CONQUER*

Goldsmith, who is said to have sung this ditty at a ladies' tea party attended by Samuel Johnson and James Boswell, had

---

@guardianstyle At a slight tangent to that, we believe in Italy football fans jeer 'arbitro cornuto' (the referee's a cuckold).

a point. In my first year at grammar school, a man named LJ Vigor taught us that Latin was 'the language of learned men', a message he was only too ready – having chalked it on to the sole of his shoe (in Latin) – to transmit to the seats of our trousers. As John Gay noted in the early 18th century, pupils were not so much taught as 'lash'd into Latin by the tingling rod'.

Don't get me wrong. Now I no longer have to study it, I quite like Latin. The Latin etymologies of many English words, and the links they reveal with other languages – that *camping it up* and *champagne*, say, are related – are fascinating. A friend taking Latin classes says 'it's like taking my brain to the gym for an hour'. The language exerts an enduring appeal, even featuring in the 1993 film *Tombstone* where Doc Holliday trades insults in Latin with Johnny Ringo, until the marshal stops them with: 'Come on boys. We don't want any trouble in here. Not in any language.'

The fun stops, however, when people who did Latin at school tell you not to use *decimate* to mean 'destroy' because in ancient Rome it meant to kill every tenth man in a mutinous group of soldiers. It's been 'wrongly used now for over 100 years', huffs Simon Heffer. He should tell the OED, which lists an example of the word in its modern sense from 1663. A *cohort* was an infantry squad in the Roman army, and I've had complaints that we should not use it to mean a small group ('the prime minister and his Cameroonian cohorts') or an aide. On that basis it's wrong to use 'legions of' to mean a lot, because a Roman legion was a division of 3,000–6,000 men. Such complaints are closely related to the 'rules' about split infinitives or prepositions that

---

@Declaniom Can evidence be a verb? 'this does not evidence your claim' – ugly but is it wrong?

were cooked up in the 18th century and taught by English teachers in thrall to Latin. As Thomas Wilson went on to say: 'The vnlearned or foolish phantasticall, that smelles but of learning (such fellowes as haue seen learned men in their daies) wil so Latin their tongues, that the simple can not but wonder at their talke, and thinke surely they speake by some reuelation.'

It's much the same with Greek. I guarantee that if we use the phrase 'the hoi polloi' in the paper, someone will write in to say that the definite article is wrong, because the ancient Greek for 'the common people' was just *hoi polloi*. But we are not writing in ancient Greek, and the phrase sounds silly without the 'the' in an English sentence. 'Brimful of learning, see that the pedant stride, bristling with horrid Greek, and puff'd with pride!' as Nicolas Boileau-Despréaux said in the 17th century.

Many Latin words have passed into English and have precise meanings that are particularly important in a legal context – eg (*exempli gratia:* 'for the sake of an example'), *in camera*, s*ine die*, *etc* (*et cetera:* 'and other things'). The English equivalent is usually simpler and clearer than its Latin counterpart – for example, 'namely' for *viz* (*videre licet:* 'one may see'). Often Latin words are misused, however: *pace*, which means 'by the leave of', sounds pompous even if used correctly – '*Pace* Simon Heffer, surely the modern use of *decimate* is simply an example of language change' – and even worse when people use it as what they imagine is a clever way to say 'such as'. *Sic* means 'so', and is normally inserted in square brackets to show that someone really did say something even though it's obviously rubbish, but should be used sparingly, as it makes you look like a know-it-all if it starts sprouting all over the place when you are quoting someone.

Latin plurals cause a lot of worry. The dangers are shown by the adoption of *alumnus* from the US instead of the traditional UK *graduate*: if you are going to use the Latin, you need to say *alumni* (male plural), *alumna* (female singular), and *alumnae* (female plural), which many people contrive to get wrong. Most Latin plurals have been adapted into English and you no more need to say *stadia* (for stadiums) or *referenda* (referendums) than you would say *musea* (museums) or *premia* (premiums). Some words do retain Latin plurals – *media*, for example. *Criteria* and *phenomena* are Greek, not Latin; there seems no particular reason to favour these plural forms – 'criterions' and 'phenomenons' sound fine to me – but no one said language was logical. Actually, lots of people did say that, but they were wrong. With 'media', a distinction can be drawn between 'TV is my favourite broadcast medium' and 'I blame the media'. Oddities include *agenda*, *data* and *dice* (the last two are related), Latin plurals normally treated as singular. A further trap to be avoided is to see a tankful of octopuses, a word of Greek origin, and call them 'octopi'. This is known as 'cod Latin'.

Finally, QED stands for *quod erat demonstrandum* – 'which was to be shown' – and is handy if you want to sound smug after winning an argument. Not to be confused with the television programme *QI*, which stands for 'Quite Interesting', or the Chinese *qi*, which means life force.

@danielle_r How would you write verb to DJ in past tense?

Americanisms? I Could Care Less

> *Society has been progressing (if I may borrow that*
> *expressive Americanism) at a very rapid rate.*
>
> MARY RUSSELL MITFORD, *OUR VILLAGE* (1824–32)

> *American idiom still, however, retained for him a secret,*
> *subtle enchantment … There was a purely aesthetic*
> *appeal … a subtle music of displaced accents, cute*
> *contractions, quaint redundancies and vivid tropes …*
> *'CIGarettes … Swiss on Rye to go … have it checked*
> *out … that's the way the cookie crumbles … '*
>
> DAVID LODGE, *CHANGING PLACES* (1975)

Today most of the controversy about the influence on British English concerns not a foreign language but a different variety of English: American English. A not untypical *Guardian* reader's letter complained: 'Your journalists are increasingly using ugly Americanisms, presumably in the belief that it is "edgy" and trendy to do so. Recent examples include *pony up, mojo, sledding, duke it out, brownstones* and *suck*, many of which are quite meaningless to me … I am not anti-American, but I do not see why our language should be corrupted by sloppy writing, and why there should be so much emphasis on all things American.' Other words complained of include *dweeb, first lady* (for the prime minister's wife), *double dip, schlepping, kindergarten*, and *authorities* ('I regard use of the term as a dreadfully ugly American import from the land without style').

@guardianstyle DJed, although it's one of those where everything looks wrong.

There is nothing new in this. In the 1950s, the *Manchester Guardian* stylebook warned against such 'Americanisms' as *balding*, *boost*, *call on the telephone*, *teen-ager* [sic] and *top secret*. I remember as a child being thrilled by early American TV shows such as *77 Sunset Strip*, demanding a crewcut (a request to which my mother, incredibly, acceded) and the right to say 'I guess' to mean 'I suppose' at every opportunity. This was widely frowned on as an American slang word too far, presumably by people unversed in Chaucer and one of his catchphrases, 'I gesse'.

As the two countries diverged, Americans retained some traditional usages that Britons lost, and vice versa. British English used to spell *cheque* 'check', as American English still does. You'd think purists would be pleased to see such respect for tradition, but no. They moan about the past participle *gotten*, which is standard in Scotland as well as the US, a remnant of Old English that survives in *ill-gotten gains*, *misbegotten*, *woebegotten*, and of course *forgotten*. You can't please some people because while they don't like *gotten* they also object to *get*, as in 'you've got mail' (rather than, if Americans were being consistent, 'you have gotten mail'). I admit that even I flinch at the increasing use of 'can I get?' instead of 'may I have?' in the UK. This, though, might just be an age thing, because no one under about 40 seems to have a problem with it at all, just as their trains go from 'train stations' while oldies like me are stuck at the railway station.

If the anti-Americanisms brigade could forget their prejudices for a moment and listen to the experts, such as Lynne Murphy (an American who teaches at a British university), they would learn that words move in both directions across

---

@colbeyuk From your guide: 'sing/pl: Nirvana were overrated'. Grammatically correct, but wrong

the Atlantic. Americans now say 'hard man' as well as tough guy, and 'ginger' as well as redhead (the *Harry Potter*, or rather Ron Weasley, effect). We Britons, meanwhile, have stepped up to the plate and adopted a wide range of US idioms. It's not cricket, you might say. It's a whole new ballgame. 'I could care less' attracts a lot of criticism – including in the US – but it's tiresome when someone says 'ah, so you *do* care!'. It's an idiom, and it's sarcastic. They couldn't care less.

So are we, as George Bernard Shaw said, 'two countries separated by a common language'? At one time it was thought that British and American English might become mutually incomprehensible, but it turns out that the problems of transatlantic communication were exaggerated. I prefer lorries to 'trucks', and I dare say some Americans are irritated by 'estate car' rather than station wagon, and we may agree to differ about suspenders, but this seems a small price to pay for a rich cultural exchange that has brought, among many others, Mark Twain, Stephen Sondheim and *Mad Men* to the UK in return for Charles Dickens, the Beatles and *Monty Python*.

Pretentious, Nous?

Of course you don't have to quote a foreign language to be pretentious. Lots of people manage it perfectly well in English, as *Private Eye*'s 'Pseuds Corner' confirms every fortnight. My own appearance in the column, which I feel was a little unfair, followed Olafur Eliasson's stunning Tate Modern installation *The Weather Project*, which featured a giant artificial sun. To accompany a review of the exhibition, one of my colleagues wrote the inspired headline 'But is it weather?' which I described as 'a work of art in its own right', thus earning my place among the pseuds.

A more recent inclusion was inspired by an interview with the singer Josh Ritter in the *Independent*, in which he chose his 'fantasy band': Edgar Allan Poe on vocals ('he's got that emo thing going on which a lot of people love'), Benjamin Franklin on keyboards ('he discovered electricity so he's a badass'), Thomas Jefferson on lead guitar ('he'd provide the eye candy'), Emily Dickinson on second guitar and to write the lyrics, and Richard III on drums. Funny or pretentious? It's a subjective thing.

Food writing readily lends itself to accusations of pomposity, as typified by Giles Coren's comment in *The Times* about sauerkraut: 'I genuinely cried at its beauty.' Talking of Giles, an email he sent after a tiny change was made to his copy has been doing the rounds of the subediting community for years. Here is an edited version:

> I wrote: 'I can't think of a nicer place to sit this spring over a glass of rosé and watch the boys and girls in the street outside smiling gaily to each other, and wondering where to go for a nosh.'
>
> It appeared as: 'I can't think of a nicer place to sit this spring over a glass of rosé and watch the boys and girls in the street outside smiling gaily to each other, and wondering where to go for nosh.'
>
> There is no length issue. This is someone thinking 'I'll just remove this indefinite article because Coren is an illiterate cunt and I know best.' Well, you fucking don't

---

@ShaunGunner Why do you not like 'per'?

... And the way you avoid this kind of fuck up is by not changing a word of my copy without asking me, okay? It's easy. Not. A. Word. Ever.

I will now explain why your error is even more shit than it looks. You see, I was making a joke. I do that sometimes ... I have used the word 'gaily' as a gentle nudge. And 'looking for a nosh' has a secondary meaning of looking for a blowjob ... I only wrote that sodding paragraph to make that joke. And you've fucking stripped it out like a pissed Irish plasterer restoring a renaissance fresco and thinking Jesus looks shit with a bear so plastering over it ...

Worst of all. Dumbest, deafest, shittest of all, you have removed the unstressed 'a' so that the stress that should have fallen on 'nosh' is lost, and my piece ends on an unstressed syllable. When you're winding up a piece of prose, metre is crucial. Can't you hear? Can't you hear that it is wrong? It's not fucking rocket science. It's fucking pre-GCSE scansion. I have written 350 restaurant reviews for 'The Times' and I have never ended on an unstressed syllable.

I woke up at three in the morning on Sunday and fucking lay there, furious, for two hours. Weird, maybe. but that's how it is.

You wouldn't want to get stuck in a restaurant with the author of such a petulant, puffed-up diatribe, even if it scans perfectly. The hapless subeditor was technically in the wrong, but may have been acting on Michael Frayn's usually reliable advice: 'Check the facts and the spelling, cross out the first sentence, and remove any attempts at jokes.'

@guardianstyle Because where possible we like the newspaper to be written in English, not Latin.

The title of this chapter is that rare thing: a punchline that is funny even without the joke. Indeed, it may be even funnier than the joke. But in case you haven't seen, or don't remember, the *Fawlty Towers* episode entitled 'The Psychiatrist', here is that joke in full (it is told by a guest, played by Nicky Henson, to a hysterical Sybil, played by Prunella Scales):

> So 'Arry says: 'You don't like me any more, why not?'
> And 'e says: 'Cos you've got so terribly pretentious.'
> And 'Arry says: 'Pretentious, moi?'

CHAPTER 8

Attack of the Jargonauts

How people in power abuse language,
and how to fight back

*We talk to our fellows in the phrases we learn from
them, which come to mean less and less as they grow
worn with use. Then we exaggerate and distort, heaping
epithet upon epithet in the endeavour to get a little
warmth out of the smouldering pile.*

SIR WALTER RALEIGH

*'I think outside the box' … 'I think inside the box' …
I'm sick and tired of all that rubbish.*

LORD SUGAR, *THE APPRENTICE* (MAY 2013)

This chapter is aimed at hard-working families. If you're a
hard-working single person or a family that doesn't work
hard – in other words, 'shirkers' – sorry: this chapter is not
for you. It's for hard-working families. And not just any
hard-working families. This is a chapter for communities.
Communities of hard-working families. Hard-working families in their communities. In a very real sense, this chapter is
about three things. Families. Communities. Hard work.

Jargon originally meant 'the inarticulate utterance of
birds, or a vocal sound resembling it; twittering, chattering';
Chaucer said someone was 'ful of Iargon as a flekked pye'

(*The Merchant's Tale*). The modern sense – defined as 'mode of speech abounding in unfamiliar terms, or peculiar to a particular set of persons, as the language of scholars or philosophers, the terminology of a science or art, or the cant of a class, sect, trade, or profession' (OED) – dates from the 17th century. So Hobbes' *Leviathan* in 1651 refers to: 'Abstract essences and substantiall formes, For the interpreting of which Iargon, there is need of somewhat more than ordinary attention.' Not much has changed in the intervening 350 years.

Bill Bryson describes jargon as 'the practice of never calling a spade a spade when you might instead call it a manual earth-restructuring implement … it is one of the great curses of modern English'. Newspapers are by no means immune from jargon, as we shall see in a later chapter. A memo sent to *Guardian* staff in April 2013 warned: 'The phishing scam impacting some *Guardian* accounts is still ongoing.'

To the jargonaut, you *alight* from, rather than get off, a train or plane. You *purchase*, rather than buy, a ticket; *endeavour*, not try; *enquire*, not ask; use *transportation*, not transport. People are *persons*. A sure sign of a jargonaut is overuse of abstract nouns, such as *actualisation*. There's nothing new about adding -*ise* to a word (*standardise* dates from the 19th century), and it can be useful – not many people would object to *privatise* (as a word). But *conceptualise* is no better than *imagine*; someone just thinks it sounds impressive. And what kind of tragic backstory can lie behind the decision to say *finalise* instead of *finish*? In theory, a word for 'put in one's diary' sounds useful, but I can't quite bring myself to write *diarise*, or even read it, without a shudder, so I'm going to stick with *schedule*.

@guardianstyle Unquestioningly is used like this:
she accepted his argument unquestioningly
(without asking any questions about it) …

I'm willing to accept *pre-paid* (paid in advance) or even *pre-order* (which carries the specific meaning that you have ordered before the item, say a CD or book, has been released or published). But we also have *pre-approved*, *pre-booked*, *preconditions*, *pre-loved*, *pre-owned*, *pre-planned*, *pre-recorded*, *pre-sliced bread*, *pre-sifted flour*, *pre-ground coffee*, *pre-shrunk jeans* and *pre-washed*. That's an awful lot of unnecessary prefixes.

Jargonauts love the passive voice. When an active sentence ('a car hit John') is passivised ('John was hit by a car'), the object of the former (John) becomes the subject, and the subject of the former (a car) becomes the object. George Orwell uses the passive repeatedly in *Animal Farm* – 'After the hoisting of the flag ... the work of the coming week *was planned out* and resolutions *were put forward* and debated' (my italics) – to create a feeling of the animals being controlled, of an inevitability about the way they behaved. We are not told who planned out 'the work of the coming week', but we can be sure it wasn't those who had to do it.

You can't just dismiss all new words, or words you don't care for, as jargon. The word *appendicitis* was initially excluded on this basis from the OED, which proved embarrassing to the editors in 1902 when Edward VII's coronation was delayed because he was suffering from 'appendicitis' and everyone wondered what it was. (As it happens, he was suffering from something else.) The word eventually made it into the OED in 1933.

URL stands for 'uniform resource locator'. Who knew? Or would want to? New technology is a ready source of jargon words, as early adopters tend to be techie types. In *Cyberspeak: An Online Dictionary* (1997), Andy Ihnatko made the point: 'The true purpose of language is to reenforce [sic] the divisions between society's tribes, or at least to make things difficult enough to understand so that the riff-raff keeps out.' In this respect, it resembles slang: when young people suddenly decided 'bad' meant 'good', what fun they had to see the confusion on their parents' faces.

Most activities – from cheerleading to churchgoing, from playing poker to playing the piccolo – develop specialist language that might not make sense to outsiders. This is all very well if the participants just need to exchange information among themselves, but the problem arises when there is a need to communicate to a wider audience. The trouble is that many people spend so much time using jargon that they lose the ability to communicate meaningfully at all. As Tom Tom Club observed, 'Who can't say what they mean, don't mean what they say.'

Things Only Get Worse: Politics-Speak

At the 2010 general election, the Liberal Democrat manifesto offered voters 'change that works for you'. Just to clarify, Nick Clegg explained that this meant 'change that will make a difference', presumably in contrast to change that makes no difference and to Gordon Brown's 'the change we choose'. Would this help 'hard-working families'? Oh yes – but not at the expense of fairness: 'People want fairness and real change' (Clegg again). Such mindless, meaningless electionspeak

---

@_MonicaAli_ Started reading the Economist Style Guide ... It's great, but little-followed I fear

brought to mind the words of Orwell: 'When one watches some tired [political] hack on the platform mechanically repeating the familiar phrases ... one often has a curious feeling that one is not watching a live human being but some kind of dummy.' That was in 1946. You might have hoped things could only get better. They didn't.

There's nothing new in the idea that politicians and civil servants use language to conceal rather than communicate. Oliver Goldsmith, echoing Voltaire, said: 'The true use of speech is not so much to express our thoughts as to conceal them.' The 19th-century Tory politician George Canning is said to have included the phrase 'he died poor' in a tribute to William Pitt the Younger. This was much too straightforward for a Whitehall official, who changed the inscription to read: 'He expired in indigent circumstances.' More than 60 years ago, newspapers were poking fun at the following unintelligible government regulation: 'In the Nuts (Unground) (Other than Groundnuts) Order, the expression nuts shall have reference to such nuts, other than groundnuts, as would, but for this Amending Order, not qualify as nuts (Unground) (Other than Groundnuts) by reason of their being nuts (Unground).'

In more recent times, Labour's 'Interception Modernisation Programme' became the coalition's 'Communications Capabilities Development Programme'. Modernisation and development: cool! What's not to like? In fact, these were plans to allow the police and security services to monitor everyone's emails and other online activities including social media, chatrooms and even computer games. My colleague Polly Toynbee warns people to look out for 'killer words [that] flash out instant red alerts: reform, flexible, harmonise and modernise all signify their opposites'. Politicians use 'reform' for a reason: it carries a positive connotation. Not many people nowadays think the Great Reform Act of 1832 was a bad idea. Hence 'NHS reforms'. A reader (a professor, in fact) accused the *Guardian* of 'colluding in this Orwellian misuse of language', adding: 'Professional conservative wordsmiths manipulate our choice of words so as to frame the debate on their terms. Your role is to expose these tactics, not collude in them.' I think he is right.

Voters will make up their own minds about whether the change that was going to make a difference made a difference for the good, the bad or the ugly under the Conservative–Liberal Democrat coalition. But as a matter of principle, one should always beware of parties with 'liberal' or 'democratic' in their name. They may turn out to be neither, as those of us who voted Lib Dem in 2010 were, alas, to discover. We also have a Conservative party that values making money above conservation (and everything else) and a Labour party most of whose MPs have never laboured at a normal job. And they wonder why people are disillusioned with politics.

John Harris of the *Guardian* suggests that the 'professionalisation' of politics is a large factor in this growing disaffection. We live in an era when if you say 'isn't it a nice day?' to a politician, they will evaluate how it will play in the tabloids before replying. If they all sound the same, it's fair to assume they are all the same. Yet politicians who say what they think rather than wait for a focus group to tell them what they think are generally popular with voters: think of the late Robin Cook on the left, or Ann Widdecombe and Nigel Farage, of the upstart UK Independence party, on the right. When Farage describes rivals as 'a bunch of college kids who've never had a proper job in their lives', it strikes a chord. Whatever you think of their views, such characters have won respect for having the courage of their convictions, notably Cook on the invasion of Iraq and Widdecombe on foxhunting. I ran the campaign for an impeccably behaved New Labour candidate at a marginal seat in the 2005 general election but it was only when she went off-message, and started to tell voters what she really believed, that she began to engage with them. It doesn't seem to occur to most politicians that there may be a connection between ever declining turnouts at elections and the rise of the android candidate, spouting jargon.

Cute Little Bomblets: Military-Speak

> President Merkin Muffley: 'You're talking about mass murder, General, not war.'
> General 'Buck' Turgidson: 'Mr President, I'm not saying we wouldn't get our hair mussed. But I do say no more than ten to twenty million killed, tops. Uh, depending on the breaks.'
>
> DR STRANGELOVE, OR HOW I LEARNED TO STOP WORRYING AND LOVE THE BOMB (STANLEY KUBRICK, 1964)

The US and its allies, notably the mindlessly loyal UK, fight wars that aren't actually wars, or winnable, such as the 'war on drugs' and the 'war on terror'. But when they actually do go to war, it's not called a war, but Operation Iraqi Freedom or, in Afghanistan, Operation Enduring Freedom. It remains to be seen how 'enduring' it is.

Minipax (the Ministry of Peace) in *Nineteen Eighty-Four* would envy the US military's mastery of its own version of Newspeak. A US Intercontinental Ballistic Missile with the destructive power of 250 Hiroshimas was 'the Peacekeeper'. Note that this was not a weapon of mass destruction – WMDs are what the bad guy has (or, in the case of Saddam Hussein, didn't have). We, of course, have a 'deterrent', although since the cold war it has been unclear who, if anyone, it is meant to deter, and from what.

The English language is abused to shield us from the reality of war and death. Killing someone on your own side becomes 'friendly fire'. Body bags are 'transfer tubes'. Kidnapping becomes 'extraordinary rendition', torture is 'enhanced interrogation techniques'. A 'surgical strike' misleadingly implies precision as well as the idea that something beneficent is being done. 'Collateral damage' means blowing people up. 'Bomblets' from cluster bombs, some dropped by UK planes despite denials by the government, lie scattered around Iraq to this day.

Large parts of the media collude in this process. Fox News reporters were instructed to call suicide bombings 'homicide bombings' to divert attention from the bomber's motives and US snipers 'sharpshooters' because of the possible negative connotations of the traditional term. Most British newspapers were cheerfully gung-ho for the Iraq invasion and no doubt will be next time. 'Terrorist suspects' tend to be presumed guilty unless found innocent.

@msjenniferjames Is it OK to say: 'I up it picked'?

Owning the Strategic Roadmap: Corporate-Speak

Barclays leadership population will be tasked and
supported to be visible exemplars and champions of
these values and behaviours.

BARCLAYS BANK CHIEF EXECUTIVE, SEPTEMBER 2012

I think he was trying to say: 'Barclays bosses will lead by example.' How refreshing it would be if business leaders were to actually use such straightforward language, instead of setting themselves up as visible exemplars of corporate verbal diarrhoea. You might wonder how people who can't speak properly can be worth millions of pounds a year to a banking sector that, after various scandals, needs more than anything else to rebuild trust with the public through effective communication. Business leaders bleat about the poor standards of literacy of young people who apply to them from school or college, but they themselves, as this and countless other examples demonstrate, seem incapable of communicating at the most basic level.

In response to criticism that copies of the *Observer* had not been available for sale at WH Smith on Waterloo station in London, the company told the newspaper's readers' editor: 'While it would appear that any shelf availability issues may only have been temporarily restricted at the time of your visit, I would also like to assure you that we do undertake various on-shelf availability checks, as part of the store compliance procedures undertaken by various members of our operations, store audit and loss-prevention teams, that operate across our estate. We have therefore reiterated the importance of these ongoing checks to our Waterloo store team and to the field staff undertaking these ongoing product availability checks, to ensure that the on-shelf availability of the *Observer* continues to be regularly checked.'

Such gibberish is everywhere in the business world. Advertisements seek managers who will 'take a dashboard approach' and 'own the strategic roadmap for the goods buying platform'. A 'specialist marketing recruitment' agency placed the following advertisement for a product manager: 'A widely renowned brand in the wealth management space is currently looking for a Product manager to take full responsibility of the electronic payments products. As the lead Product Manager for Electronic payments you will be fully responsible for the proposition and the development for a variety of Payment solutions to enable growth opportunity for the organisation globally.' As the successful candidate was to be paid up to £70,000 a year, hopefully they understood this drivel.

Corporate types are obsessed with growth, and in particular with 'growing the business'. Like many jargonauts, they are also very keen on 'delivery'. Sometimes their message is almost incomprehensible: this slogan appeared in an office window, below the name of a London company:

Delivering actionable insight in a multi channel world

In the vain hope of deciphering this, I visited their website, which offers help 'whether your business is B2C, B2B, B2B2C or is considering going direct to consumer (D2C) for the first time'. 'Delivery', very popular in Whitehall and local government as well as business, is a dead giveaway that

---

@BeatriceJBray I was asked out by a sub for dinner. He spent the whole time proofreading the menu & not talking to me

you have come up against a jargonaut. At least it saves you from bothering to read the rest of what will be a meaningless or incomprehensible message. Other words to run a mile from include 'ongoing', 'proactive' and the dreaded 'synergy'.

Straightforward words like 'before' and 'more than' have been expunged from the corporate vocabulary to be replaced by 'prior to' or 'ahead of' and 'in excess of'. Future events are 'upcoming' and today's busy executive is always 'going forward'. They no longer speak about things, but speak 'to' them. As in: 'I can't speak to market conditions in east Asia, but I know things are tough in Europe right now.' The business jargonaut does not engage in talks, but 'dialogue' or, even worse, 'meaningful dialogue', a phrase which Kingsley Amis rightly said 'unerringly points out its user as a humourless ninny'.

The communications agency Doris & Bertie – named after Warren Buffett's sisters, because the investor is 'well known for his down-to-earth communication style' and 'writes all his business documents as if he were talking to his sisters' – has a blog called Good Copy, Bad Copy, devoted to exposing 'bad business writing'. Here is an example:

> *The objective of the assessment was to conduct a surveillance assessment and look for positive evidence to ensure that elements of the scope of certification and the requirements of the management standard are effectively addressed by the organisation's management system and that the system is demonstrating the ability to support the achievement of statutory, regulatory and contractual requirements and the organisations [sic] specified objectives, as applicable with regard to the scope of the*

*management standard, and to confirm the on-going
achievement and applicability of the forward strategic
plan and where applicable to identify potential areas for
improvement of the management system.*

Perhaps this should have gone in the previous chapter, about foreign languages.

Queue Here to Respect Patients: NHS-Speak

*Like many hospitals, we're experiencing language
problems with some nursing staff ... not enough of them
speak management!*

CARTOON BY FRAN, *PRIVATE EYE*

The National Health Service (NHS) may be doing a great job, and hopefully will continue to do so despite the government's 'reforms', but it is no thanks to the jargonauts. The following extract was one of four NHS 'winners' of the Plain English Campaign's Golden Bull awards in 2012.

*A unique factor of the NHS Cheshire Warrington and
Wirral Commissioning support organisation is its
systematised methodology for project and programme
management of small, medium, large service re-design
and implementation ... Building in equality and risk
impact assessments the options are taken through a process
to arrive at the content for an output based specification
and benefits foreseen as a result of the implementation.*

@RichardA Check out @guardianstyle – currently dispensing quirky British linguistic usage

> *The service is inclusive of full engagement with Clinical Commissioning Groups who direct at decision-making points how they wish the proposal to be deployed (re-commmisson [sic], de-commission or changes to current services/providers), and lastly an implementation team who see the service redesign through to evaluation and benefits realisation.*

A sign outside Lloyds, the pharmacy at one of my local hospitals – or 'Lloydspharmacy' as it chooses to style itself – says:

> *Please wait here to hand*
> *in prescriptions &*
> *to respect the privacy of*
> *other patients.*
> *We will serve you as soon as possible.*
> *Thankyou.*

You can see what they were trying to do here. The idea is that while waiting to hand in prescriptions we should respect the privacy of other patients. That little word 'to', however, has sabotaged the whole thing. You just can't get two thoughts into one sentence by randomly sticking in a short word that might or might not (in this case, not) connect them. And when and why 'thankyou' became one word I am not sure. Why didn't someone read the notice out loud?

> *Please wait here to hand in prescriptions.*
> *Please respect the privacy of other patients.*
> *We will serve you as soon as possible.*
> *Thank you.*

@guardianstyle 'Currently'? You think we are going to stop?

There is nothing difficult about my version of the sign. It's clearer, simpler, more polite, and reflects the way the perpetrators might communicate with people in a normal way when not engaged in their professional capacity of communicating with people by writing signs for 'Lloydspharmacy'.

We Do Apologise: Rail-Speak

A malign side-effect of the John Major government's botched sell-off of the UK railway system in the 1990s was the language that commuters are forced to listen to as they suffer in conditions that would lead lambs heading for the abattoir to write to their MP. Railspeak is a variety of language with its own syntax and vocabulary – characterised by the mandatory use of auxiliary verbs ('we do apologise' – a jargonaut's favourite), the random deployment of redundant adjectives ('*station* stop', '*personal* belongings'), and the choice of inappropriate prepositions ('journey time *into* London Paddington is approximately 25 minutes'). Trains do not leave, but 'depart', never reach their destination, but 'terminate', and are frequently delayed by mysterious 'incidents'. Train catering, meanwhile, has been transformed from a music hall joke (British Rail sandwiches) to a surreal world of its own, offering among other treats 'teas, coffees, hot chocolates [sic] … ' I wonder if anyone has tested this by asking how many varieties of hot chocolate are, in fact, available.

The effect of all this is to create a gulf between the language used by railspeakers and those on the receiving end. Calling

@burntoutcar Crematoriums??! Really? Even though it's stadia and auditoria? How so?

people 'standard-class customers' will alienate them if the reality is that they feel treated like second-class passengers. Hyper-correct, hyper-polite language may be well intended but comes across as patronising and insincere. I do not blame the people who have to make these announcements. They don't write them themselves; someone sitting in an office does that. I have not seen a policeman on a train since the days of football specials in the 1970s, yet we are told several times on every journey to report anything suspicious to the train manager 'or a police officer'. Nor have I met a fellow passenger – sorry, customer – who does not find 'arriving into' very annoying. Why not say 'arriving at' and make the world a happier place?

The language of announcements is counterproductive. People infuriated by non-stop 'customer security information', constantly being told not to leave their 'personal luggage, cases and parcels' unattended (are you supposed to take it with you to the 'express cafe'?) and repeatedly being reminded that 'this is a non-smoking service' (we know) will retreat into their iPods, still known as 'personal stereos' in railspeak, and not listen to any information at all. So when there is something important to announce – the train is on fire, say – no one will hear.

In the meantime, someone should tell station announcers that the ever lengthening list of things we can't do – smoke, run, cycle, skateboard, find a rubbish bin, find a seat – does not, so far, extend to playing boules or yodelling. Is this an oversight?

@guardianstyle It's stadiums and auditoriums too.

Hyper Unreality: Artists and Academics

International Art English (IAE) is a term devised by David Levine, an artist, and Alix Rule, a critic, who analysed language used in press releases and galleries and concluded that IAE is a 'unique language' that has 'everything to do with English, but is emphatically not English'. Characteristics include using more rather than fewer words, and employing words to 'take on non-specific alien functions' such as the essentially meaningless 'reality functions as my field of action' (artist Tania Bruguera). As with other forms of jargon, they say its importance to those who use it is that it confirms their insider status.

Academics are even worse. In my first reporting job, straight out of university, it took six months for the news editor to cure me of writing 10 long words where five short ones would do, a habit I had acquired in a successful attempt to make my essays sound more impressive to the examiner. When I went back to university to do a master's 25 years later, it took six months for my tutor to cure me of writing five short words where 10 long ones would do.

There are of course exceptions, some of which are listed at the back of this book, but open most academic textbooks at random and you don't have to go very far to realise that the author has lost, or chosen not to use, any ability to communicate clearly and simply with the reader. I dare say this is inevitable in fields such as astrophysics. But if it's not rocket science – when it's economics, say, or language – there seems no excuse for making things harder for the sake of it.

@unit01 Why are two spaces following a period no longer necessary?

Just take a look at this abstract from a recent Oxford University economics research paper (quoted in *Private Eye*'s 'Pseuds Corner'): 'We show that such thresholds are nonparametrically identified from standard admissions data if unobserved officers' heterogeneity affecting admission decisions is median-independent of applicant covariates and the density of past admits' [sic] conditional expected performance is positive around the admission threshold for each socio-economic group.' I believe it is about university admission procedures, but I might have got my covariates mixed up.

Deceptive Gibberish: Estate Agents

Estate agents have maintained the 18th-century tradition of using capital letters for almost all nouns, so that looking through the descriptions of houses in one's local paper is rather like reading Alexander Pope: 'Located In One Of Newbury's Foremost Residential Addresses. £999,995.' I suppose at that price they think they should include all those capital letters. At least the apostrophe is in the right place, unlike this one: 'The delightful gardens that adjoin this property are without doubt one of it's most redeeming features and measure approximately 0.75 acre in total.' Would you buy a house from someone who doesn't know what 'redeeming' means?

They may have one eye on the past, but estate agents (like all jargonauts) are always on the lookout for new ways to irritate people. Thus did semi-detached become 'attached', perhaps because it sounds more like 'detached' and they think buyers might not notice their new home is joined to someone else's until they move in. Estate agents are also very fond of the word 'deceptively', as in 'deceptively spacious', which I think means 'not as small as it looks' although the word is ambiguous: in a survey, half the respondents thought 'deceptively easy' meant easy, and half thought it meant hard. It is, therefore, rarely used by normal people.

The term 'affordable homes', which to be fair is more the responsibility of local authorities than estate agents, leads to this kind of nonsense, from a news story in my local paper: 'Developer wants permission for 40 homes but says it doubts any will be affordable.' The mistake arises because of the ambiguity of affordable in the sense of 'can be afforded' and the newer jargon sense of something like 'can be afforded by people on low incomes'. The result is absurdity.

Unspeak

Steven Poole, a *Guardian* colleague, coined this term to categorise language that conceals what the speaker really means, 'smuggling in' an opinion in which 'a whole partisan argument is packed into a soundbite', while at the same time attempting to rubbish one's opponents by suggesting that there is only one way of looking at an issue. Examples he gives include 'pro-life' and 'pro-choice' in the abortion debate (who could possibly not be in favour of life and choice?). He analyses the successful campaign to replace the term global warming with the vaguer and less frightening climate change, and how intelligent design was adopted by creationists in the US; both terms were then used in attempts

---

@zoelouwhite Please oh wise one, advisor or adviser?

to discredit science, suggesting that global warming and evolution were controversial theories and that there remains a genuine 'debate' about such issues.

Getting back to election campaigns, that of 2005 – when Michael Howard's Conservatives took on Tony Blair's Labour party not long after the Iraq war – marked a low point with the Tories' poster campaign 'It's not racist to impose limits on immigration' coupled with the subtext in capital letters 'ARE YOU THINKING WHAT WE'RE THINKING?' This might be paraphrased 'we are racist, just like you, but we're not allowed to say so', according to Poole, who calls it 'a brilliant piece of Unspeak – the hate that dares not speak its name'. As it turned out, the voters wanted nothing to do with it. If the price of abandoning such nastiness was the bland drivel about 'change' and 'hard-working families' that we were served up five years later, then I suppose it was worth paying.

How to Fight Back

This chapter is not a rant against declining standards of English or a harking back to some imagined golden age. Orwell was complaining eloquently about the misuse of language by politicians more than 80 years ago. People in authority have always used language in an attempt to assert their supposed superiority, and there have always been others to criticise or make fun of them. Note that 'people in authority'. Ordinary people have little time for jargon in their everyday lives, unless it is relevant to their job or leisure interests. Yet they have to face this alienating barrage of gobbledegook from all sides,

@guardianstyle Both in dictionary, but we prefer adviser (and same for protester).

including areas I've not covered, such as the law. No wonder so many refuse to engage with politicians, regard bankers, business leaders and bureaucrats with contempt, become frustrated in their communications with organisations such as the NHS that they fund through their taxes, and can't even catch a train without being subjected to gibberish cooked up by a remote private company.

It's not easy to counter this. Steven Poole says the media should not uncritically accept this language – agreed – but then says people should 'talk back: write and tell them', which seems a bit weak. Perhaps we need a language equivalent of Mary Portas, the retail expert given the task of saving our recession-ravaged high streets. Such a person could advise public bodies, supermarkets and other businesses how to smarten up and simplify the way they communicate with the public. I am available.

There are a few other things we could try. Resolve not to vote for any politician who talks to you as if your cat has just died, or refuses to give a straight answer to a straight question. Post political propaganda back to the party that sent it you if it is not written in an honest and straightforward way. Write back to companies that send you ambiguous, badly written or sloppy letters, asking them to explain what they mean in plain English. Above all, don't get sucked in. Be as clear as you can in your own communications, spoken or written, formal or informal. If we all do that, perhaps one day those in power will realise that it might be in their interests to do the same. Because no one is listening.

CHAPTER 9

Political Incorrectness Gone Mad

Writers who rant against 'political correctness' are just bad losers

> *If the English language had been properly organised ... there would be a word which meant both 'he' and 'she', and I could write: 'If John or May comes, heesh will want to play tennis,' which would save a lot of trouble.*
>
> AA MILNE, *THE CHRISTOPHER ROBIN BIRTHDAY BOOK*

> *How, in a cultural climate in which there's no clear line between simple courtesy and a violation of constitutional rights, do you know how to choose your words? How can you be sure to never offend anyone with inadvertently sexist or racist language? That's easy: just don't speak or write anything ever.*
>
> JUNE CASAGRANDE, *GRAMMAR SNOBS ARE GREAT BIG MEANIES*

During a parliamentary debate in May 2013 on proposals to allow couples of the same sex to marry, the Conservative MP Edward Leigh said: 'Mild-mannered people expressing reasonable beliefs in moderate tones are treated like villains.' And why? We live in a culture 'so coloured by political correctness' that the 'outlandish views of the loony left of the 1980s' are now 'embedded in high places'.

In the same debate, the Labour MP David Lammy recalled how within living memory the 'Windrush generation' of immigrants had arrived in Britain to be greeted by signs in windows saying: 'No Irish, no blacks, no dogs.' That was now illegal and future generations, he suggested, might regard not allowing gay people to marry as in the same category of bigotry and intolerance.

On the face of it, the divisions could not be starker. Although the issue was same-sex marriage, to Leigh it was all part of an assault on British values, an onslaught best summed up by the phrase 'political correctness'. Traditionalists often resort to this phrase as a catch-all explanation for things they don't like or understand about the modern world. It's all the fault of the 'PC brigade'. Grammar is no longer taught in our schools. Exams have been 'dumbed down'. Hit a child these days and someone is likely to accuse you of assault. Prison is a soft touch. That fine old world 'gay' has been hijacked by homosexualists. These PC wimmin would have us saying 'personhole' instead of manhole. You can't say what you think any more for fear of breaking the European convention on human rights.

In plain language that they should be able to appreciate, allow me to reply to the 'anti-PC brigade' brigade with a good old-fashioned – in fact Old English – word.

Beallucs!

Just as most people (including, it turns out, a majority of MPs and peers) are relaxed about same-sex marriage, most people recognise that nowadays there are things you should and should not say, and it mainly boils down to consideration for others. Is this such a terrible burden? Only, it seems, for a minority of politicians and their supporters

@NadVega So being a woman is now a stigma? Just great.

in newspapers. Given the amount of space devoted to the imagined scourge of 'political correctness', it's surprising that people aren't more agitated about it. Perhaps they realise that, in the words of my colleague Polly Toynbee, 'politically correct' is 'an empty rightwing smear designed only to elevate its user'.

Every Man for Him or Herself

How often he had spoken scornfully of that word 'lady'!
Were not all of the sex women? What need for that
hateful distinction?

GEORGE GISSING, *DEMOS* (1886)

Most sexist and racist language arises from the presumption that everyone is male and white. If you can just remember that this is not, in fact, the case, sexist and racist language is easy to avoid.

As long ago as 1911, the American writer Ambrose Bierce, in his satirical *The Devil's Dictionary*, objected to Miss – 'a title with which we brand unmarried women to indicate that they are in the market' – and proposed that for consistency there should be a title for the unmarried man: 'I venture to suggest Mush, abbreviate to Mh.' We may have to wait a while longer for 'Mh', but Ms, which I recall being greeted with ridicule when it started to catch on in the 1960s and 70s, is now well established. The assumption that women's marital status, but not men's, should be included in the formal way they are identified is rightly becoming a thing of the past.

@guardianstyle Of course not, but being called a 'career girl' might be.

Some men just do not have the grace to admit they are beaten. The fact that the deputy leader of one of our main political parties is female and has the word 'man' in her name is an endless source of amusement to the kind of person who thinks it witty to call her 'Harriet Harperson'. Well, it saves them having to engage with issues such as the Church of England's refusal to tolerate female bishops. One columnist wrote in the *Daily Mail*: 'What next? Perhaps, as she plots her own takeover of the Labour party leadership, Harman is even now planning legislation that at least one contender for the next Archbishop of Canterbury will have to wear a skirt.' Dismissing Harman as a 'zealot', in the same column the writer defended someone who described gay men as 'sodomites' whose 'perverted sexual practices' were responsible for spreading sexually transmitted diseases.

Such drivel is, sadly, churned out by all too many men (and, inexplicably, some women). Why would anyone want to subject herself to this? No wonder fewer than one in three Labour MPs, one in six Tory MPs and one in eight Liberal Democrat MPs are female. The Conservative party, of course, has had two female 'chairmen' in recent years, which is up to them. Many organisations favour 'chair', although 'chairwoman' sounds fine to me, as does 'spokeswoman' as an equivalent to 'spokesman'. I'd save 'person' for cases where you don't know the person's sex: chairperson and spokesperson have a touch of jargon about them, although both are still far preferable to treating women as an afterthought.

Within not much more than a couple of decades, policemen and woman police constables have become police officers, firemen are now firefighters, male nurses are nurses,

---

@miss_silva Jane & Joss' party/Jane & Joss's party/Joss's party/Joss' party/?

postmen are postal workers, air hostesses have become cabin crew. In all these cases, language reflects the fact that jobs once largely the preserve of one sex are now increasingly filled by either. 'Career girls' is outdated, as well as offensive, when career women outnumber career men. Opponents of such modest but significant changes respond with feeble jokes about non-existent proposals to 'person the barricades' and the like. It's not so long ago that female doctors were rare enough to be given the description 'lady doctor'. Sexist habits persist in using 'woman' as an adjective in such phrases as 'woman bishop' and 'women MPs', with their pejorative echo of 'women drivers'. You don't hear anyone described as a 'man MP', but then that's what most MPs always have been.

What the American author Bryan A Garner has described as the single biggest problem in sexist language is the generic masculine pronoun. The language simply lacks an 'epicene' (gender-neutral) equivalent of he and she. The traditional remedy has been to treat everyone as if they were male, and use 'he' to cover both, or resort to clumsy constructions like 'he or she' or 'his/her'. But wait ...

> 'If everybody minded their own business,' said The
> Duchess in a hoarse growl, 'the world would go round a
> deal faster than it does.'
>
> LEWIS CARROLL, *ALICE'S ADVENTURES IN WONDERLAND*

Note that Carroll, writing in 1865, did not write 'his own business' or 'his or her own business'. The use of the singular 'their' is too much for the likes of Simon Heffer, 150 years later, who writes in *Strictly English*: 'I regard that as abominable and

---

@guardianstyle Could Joss and Jane be persuaded to help us all out here and hold their party at someone else's?

want no part of it.' As well as Lewis Carroll, this presumably makes Shakespeare, the Bible and Thackeray, in Heffer's words, 'simply illiterate':

> *There's not a man I meet but doth salute me.*
> *As if I were their well-acquainted friend.*
> WILLIAM SHAKESPEARE, *THE COMEDY OF ERRORS*

> *If ye from your hearts forgive not every one his brother*
> *their trespasses ...*
> MATTHEW 18:35 (AUTHORISED VERSION)

> *A person can't help their birth.*
> WILLIAM MAKEPEACE THACKERAY, *VANITY FAIR*

If they can do it, so can you. English, after all, used to have a singular version of 'you' – *thee*, *thou* and *thy* – and it is still heard in some dialects (at the football in Sheffield, it is perfectly normal to hear someone shouting 'tha [thou] needs tha [thy] glasses, ref!'). 'You' gradually squeezed these words out to become standard for singular as well as plural, and no great anguish seems to have been caused, even in Yorkshire. There is no reason why something similar should not happen to 'they'. Singular 'they' or 'their' is much less clumsy than 'he or she' or 'his or her', and does not consign half the human race to subservience by calling women 'he'.

Indefinite pronouns – anyone, everyone, somebody, someone or whoever – are grammatically singular but often have a plural reference, and so can take plural pronouns. This

---

@guardianstyle Mail takes #iconwatch prize for most 'iconics' this week: red deer, The Birth of Venus, Philip Treacy's hats, José Mourinho, Jaguar car ...

is known as notional agreement. Anyone can do it if they want. And if everyone who agrees can please raise their hand, I will move on.

Actors and Doctresses

Doll Common doing Abigail most excellent, &
Knipp the widow very well, & will be an excellent actor,
I think.
SAMUEL PEPYS, DIARY, 27 DECEMBER 1666

An actress can only play a woman. I'm an actor: I can
play anything.
WHOOPI GOLDBERG

If I describe the late Hattie Jacques as the finest actress in the *Carry On* films, I am judging her against the likes of Joan Sims, Barbara Windsor and (the criminally underrated) Patsy Rowlands. If I declare her to be the finest *Carry On* actor, I am saying Hattie's body of work was not just better than the other women's, but superior to those of Kenneth Williams, Sidney James and Charles Hawtrey as well. This seems so obvious to me – the language, not necessarily the best actor – that I am surprised that calling male and female actors 'actors', a policy I introduced to the *Guardian*, caused anyone to raise an eyebrow. It has upset a few people, however. To put the controversy in perspective, I received 20 complaints (all but two from men) in the first 10 years of the

----

@**guardianstyle** More Mail 'iconics': the Skerryvore lighthouse, a woman's pear-shaped figure ... is there nothing these people don't find iconic? #iconwatch

policy. I asked them if they mourned the passing of words like authoress, poetess and sculptress, which were still around when I was young.

Perhaps the complainants would agree with HW Fowler, who in 1926 proposed a set of new 'feminine vocation-words' in a well-intentioned, if misjudged, response to the increase of women in the workplace. He argued: 'Everyone knows the inconvenience of being uncertain whether a doctor is a man or a woman; hesitation in establishing the word *doctress* is amazing in a people regarded as nothing but practical. Far from needing to reduce the number of our sex-words, we should do well to indulge in real neologisms such as *teacheress*, *singeress* and *danceress*.'

The idea failed to catch on, although the feminine suffixes *-ess*, *-enne* or *-ette* used to be common enough. But such words reflect a different era, suggesting that the masculine is the norm. I think actress comes into the same category as comedienne, manageress, usherette and similar largely obsolete terms that date from a time when such roles were largely the preserve of one sex. Today there is no need to differentiate between the sexes – and if there is, the words male and female are perfectly adequate: Lady Gaga won a Brit for best international female artist, not artiste, chanteuse or songstress. Harriet Walter is, and was described as such in the *Guardian*, 'one of our finest stage actors'. And guys, that includes you.

The Ethnic Population

> *'He admits to having abandoned 20 men to their*
> *deaths.'*
> *'They were only natives ... '*
> *'Black or white, they are our brothers.'*
> *Vera thought: 'Our black brothers – our black brothers.*
> *Oh, I'm going to laugh.'*
>
> AGATHA CHRISTIE, *AND THEN THERE WERE NONE*

Spoiler alert: anyone who has been living on Mars for the last 50 years should skip the next sentence. Agatha Christie was too busy catching a wave – she was one of the first surfers – and generally having a good time to spend much time on her writing technique, but what she lacked in style she more than made up for in her ingenious plots (the policeman did it, the narrator did it, one of the victims did it, they all did it).

Christie's most successful book (and the seventh biggest-selling book by anyone, ever) was published as *Ten Little Niggers* in 1939 and retained that title in the UK until the 1980s. In the US it was published in 1940 as *And Then There Were None*. The Ten Little Niggers nursery rhyme, on which the plot centres, has been – variously – Ten Little Indians, Ten Little Soldiers and – in the computer game version – Ten Little Sailor Boys.

As recently as the 1973 edition of Eric Partridge's *Usage and Abusage*, the advice about 'nigger' was that it 'belongs only, and then only in contempt or fun, to the dark-skinned

---

@guardianstyle And let's not forget 'the iconic wandering albatross' (Times) #iconwatch (with thanks to @ JulieParkJersey) – another clichewatch next Friday

African races and their descendants in American and the West Indies. Its application to the native peoples of India is ignorant and offensive.'

We have moved on since the days of such casual racism. Just as police officers can be male or female, offenders are no longer necessarily presumed to be from an ethnic minority, as when descriptions of suspects failed to mention their race if they were white. But you still see newspapers lazily using the adjective 'ethnic' (which, of course, we all are) to mean minority ethnic in such expressions as 'ethnic population'.

There are plenty of other examples of media coverage that, wittingly or not, promote division and play into the hands of extremists. An asylum seeker is someone seeking refugee status or humanitarian protection. There is no such thing as an 'illegal asylum seeker', a term that even the dozy and discredited Press Complaints Commission ruled in breach of its code of practice. Someone who has been refused asylum is a refused asylum seeker, not a 'failed' or 'bogus' asylum seeker.

The immigration debate, which does nothing to enhance the UK's reputation for tolerance at the best of times, is twisted by misuse of the very word 'immigrant', used negatively for so many years and often incorrectly applied to people who were born in Britain. Terms like 'second-generation immigrants' suggest that such people are not fully 'one of us' when a neutral and more accurate term, 'children of immigrants', is readily available.

@oflynnexpress What about style icon 'Wallace' Simpson on p1 of the Guardian the other day?

Hello in Normal Land

> *'Disabled' is a label that hurts ... Imagine that each day*
> *of your life you were forced to face that label, exactly as*
> *we once forced black people, with labels on every aspect*
> *of their being – restrooms, restaurants, hotels, seating on*
> *a bus ... and you will have some understanding of how*
> *words hurt.*

HAROLD MAIO

In 2012 the British Paralympic Association produced a guide for reporting on Paralympic sport that is a model of enlightened common sense. Its advice can be usefully applied to more than just athletics. 'Nothing irritates world-class Paralympic athletes more than being patronised or pitied, or made to feel that their impairment is being utilised ultimately to define them or their achievements,' it says.

While an athlete's impairment should be mentioned only if essential – because it is irrelevant to their achievements – the guide does suggest preferred terms:

- disabled person (not 'person with a disability');
- non-disabled person (not 'able-bodied', 'normal');
- a person/athlete who has a spinal cord injury or a person/ athlete with paraplegia (not 'a spinal injury athlete', 'a paraplegic');
- a wheelchair user or person who uses a wheelchair (not 'wheelchair-bound', 'confined to a wheelchair').

@guardianstyle Was she in Wallis & Gromit?

Among further phrases to avoid, it lists:

- suffers from, afflicted with, victim of (athletes do not want to be portrayed as weak, frail or tragic);
- the disabled, the blind (grouping disabled people by their disability in this way implies all disabled people in that group share the same characteristics, which stereotypes them);
- abnormal, defective or deformed (adjectives with negative connotations);
- spastic, retard, handicap, invalid and cripple (nouns with negative connotations);
- normal (highly subjective, especially in a sporting context – 'would you describe Chris Hoy or Usain Bolt as "normal"?' ['Hello in Normal Land', as Ian Dury sardonically put it in 'Spasticus Autisticus'.]

Finally, the guide says there is no need to feel conscious about using everyday phrases: 'Some people who use wheelchairs will state themselves "I'm going for a walk". It is also perfectly acceptable to say to a visually impaired person "I will see you later".'

The phrase 'basket case' dates from the US in 1919, originally referring to quadriplegics who had suffered catastrophic wounds in the first world war. The more recent figurative sense of someone who is emotionally unable to cope dates from 1967. Nowadays it is chiefly used to describe economies that are not functioning properly, particularly when Europhobic newspapers write about other EU countries. Is it offensive? A reader thought so: 'It is a shocking, distressing and distracting image. Its power derives from the notion that a double amputee is useless and their existence unsustainable. Even if this were true (which it isn't), the metaphor would still be better avoided.' I agree, and we do avoid it.

The Myth of 'Political Correctness'

There are those, and not only the usual suspects, who sneer at such advice. The otherwise tolerant Robert Allen in *How to Write Better English* criticises the 'rejection' of words such as manhandle and (of course) manhole which, so far as I am aware, no one seriously objects to. Declaring that 'political correctness represents an extreme', he continues: 'Backward and educationally subnormal become intellectually challenged; short becomes vertically challenged; and disabled becomes physically challenged.' (Who has ever, other than ironically, suggested 'vertically challenged' as an alternative to short?) The politically correct, he says, seek to replace failure with 'achievement deficiency' and disabled with 'differently abled'. Oh really? This is the linguistic equivalent of accusing Labour councils of banning Baa Baa Black Sheep for being racist or banning conkers for 'health and safety' reasons. It is rubbish.

Even David Crystal, in *Who Cares About English Usage?* – a book that makes repeated pleas for linguistic tolerance – says: 'When you see the lengths people are prepared to go, to avoid sexist criticism of any kind, it's difficult to keep a straight face' – his examples include such rib-ticklers as craftsperson (instead of craftsman), postperson (instead of postman) and humankind (instead of mankind).

@guardianstyle Referendums
(in Latin, referendum has no plural).

I find such attitudes desperately disappointing. Language decried as 'PC' has made our society more civilised. A decade on, it's hard to imagine a headline like the *Sun*'s 'BONKERS BRUNO LOCKED UP', above a story that went on to describe the boxer as 'nuts', appearing now. One in four people will have some form of mental illness at some stage in their lives and it was the public outcry that led to a climbdown. There are still all too many 'psychos' and 'schizos' in the tabloids, however, while as recently as 2010 a *Guardian* columnist contrived to accuse the Conservatives of 'untreatable ideological schizophrenia'. Such terms should be reserved purely for the medical condition. Autism is a neurological disorder, not a term of abuse or a source of such witticisms as 'Star Wars is a form of male autism'. Figurative use of serious medical conditions should be no more acceptable than terms such as cripple, lunatic and spastic, which became terms of abuse for others. It comes as a surprise that Scope did not change its name from the Spastics Society until 1994.

While it's always a pleasure to be attacked by headbangers who shout first and think (if at all) later, a piece that Rod Liddle wrote in the *Spectator* asking 'Why has the word "grandmother" been banned by the *Guardian*?' was a tendentious piece of 'anti-PC' twaddle. Nothing has been banned. I simply advise our writers to mention that someone is a grandparent only when relevant, and to 'leave "battling grannies" and other examples of ageism and sexism to the tabloids'. We also think terms such as 'OAP' are old-fashioned and irrelevant when you can be running a marathon, a business or indeed a country long past traditional retirement age.

@martingowans What happens after style mistakes are noticed in published articles?

Liddle (a former *Guardian* columnist) gave a long list of other words and phrases he would like to see in the paper but which I had 'banned', such as 'active homosexual', 'career woman', 'committed suicide', 'crippled', 'handicapped', 'hare lip', 'Siamese twins', 'spinster' and 'illegal asylum seeker'. While Rod is not responsible for the comments under his blog, *Spectator* readers sound like a lovely bunch: I am a Marxist, engaged in 'thought control experiments' funded by the taxpayer (how?), 'deconstructing the English language, as well as the rest of our culture'. I need hardly add that in no time at all similar columnists such as Stephen Glover were accusing me of – yes – 'political correctness'.

I think they are just bad losers. Even if it has not led to universally tolerant attitudes, sensitive language has been a force for good in recent decades. Just think about how people with Down's syndrome, say, are regarded now compared with when they were labelled 'mongols'. Having a disability need not 'cripple' your life, make you 'invalid' or prove an insurmountable 'handicap'. People who would have been written off by previous generations are now recognised as having an equal stake in society. Being thoughtful and sensitive about the language you use is not hard; opening your mind to change, for some people, is. But don't let them fool you. 'Political correctness' is a myth. It's political incorrectness gone mad.

CHAPTER 10

I Fed the Newts Today, Oh Boy

What I've learned from 40 years in newspapers
– and the best headline of all time

> *You cannot hope to bribe or twist*
> *Thank God! The British journalist.*
> *But seeing what the man will do*
> *Unbribed, there's no occasion to.*
>
> HUMBERT WOLFE

> *Journalists say a thing that they know isn't true in the*
> *hope that if they keep saying it long enough it will be true.*
>
> ARNOLD BENNETT

'Fact × Importance = News' was the formula on Channel 4's *The Day Today* (a programme that looks less and less like satire the more you compare it with real broadcasts). The truth, as ever, is a little more complicated. So what is news? Non-journalists often assume, reasonably enough, that the number of pages in a newspaper is decided by the amount of news that is around on any given day. In fact, it is entirely dictated by the amount of advertising that has been sold; the only exception I have come across in four decades was on 11 September 2001, when we dropped all advertising from the paper.

You may recall that day as the one when New Labour, and modern politics in general, hit a nadir from which they have never recovered when a special adviser sent a memo at 2.55pm, as people were watching the twin towers collapse, saying – and as someone who was a Labour party member for 30 years, I am embarrassed to type this – 'It is now a very good day to get out anything we want to bury. Councillors' expenses?' While shameful, this episode illustrates my point: the amount of coverage given to a story rests on what else is happening at least as much as on its own importance. Aldous Huxley and CS Lewis, two great British authors who died on 22 November 1963, would have received rather more coverage had President John F Kennedy not been assassinated on the same day.

Although such momentous, if rare, stories will always dominate media coverage, it is a misconception that there is a finite amount of 'news' out there and that the journalist's role is to try to 'capture' it. An honest definition of news would be: *news is whatever journalists say it is*. Freddie Starr eating a hamster (guess what: he didn't really) can be news to one paper. A footballer's wife going to the supermarket is news to another. What amounted to collusion between elements of the press, the police and the politicians to cover up claims that people's phones were being routinely hacked into was news for years, but only according to one newspaper.

Journalists come somewhere near the bottom of the popularity charts, just above politicians, and we probably have ourselves, or perhaps the people we choose to work for, to blame. Much of the good in journalism has been overshadowed by the bad and the downright ugly. People might

---

@RobertShippey What's correct? email, eMail, e-mail ?
< Good question for @guardianstyle

have understood phone hacking if it had been about exposing corruption, not cruel intrusion into the lives of crime victims and tawdry tittle-tattle about celebrities. Gossip – 'a sort of smoke that comes from the dirty tobacco-pipes of those who diffuse it: it proves nothing but the bad taste of the smoker', as George Eliot put it – has replaced serious news in the redtops as they try to repeat the formula, without much of the flair, of a great editor like, loathe him or loathe him, Kelvin MacKenzie.

Papers' prejudices, or those of their owners, render impossible any kind of serious discussion about, say, immigration or the UK's future in Europe. Columnists, particularly on the midmarket tabloids, are too often, in my colleague Charlie Brooker's phrase, 'people who waste their lives actively making the world worse'. Yet it is a newspaper that exposes the secret of how the US spies on its own citizens with a rigour that the East German Stasi would have envied. From the thalidomide scandal to MPs' expenses, from Hillsborough to tax avoidance, British newspapers have a proud record of uncovering abuse of power and, often, criminal activity.

An Elephant Never Forgets a Cliche

> *The life of a journalist is poor, nasty, brutish and short.*
> *So is his style.*
>
> STELLA GIBBONS, *COLD COMFORT FARM*

If you were wondering why the media managed to get off scot-free in the chapter about jargon, wonder no more.

Why, jargon and cliches are our very lifeblood. My quest for perfection, or at least an improvement, in the spelling and grammar of the *Guardian* has been more successful than my attempts to curb the use of hackneyed phrases. People tend to associate journalese – a language found only in newspapers – with the tabloids. And it's true that very few people in real life talk about jobs being 'axed' or given a 'massive boost', discuss the latest police 'bid' to 'probe' a crime, suffer traffic or weather-related 'misery', or have 'pals' who reveal their innermost thoughts. Such language, far from adding drama, can have a deadening effect.

After 25 years on what we used to call broadsheets, or what Kelvin MacKenzie describes as 'the unpopular press', I can assure you we also have our own style of language that bears only a tangential relationship to the way normal people speak. Bill Bryson says: 'Anyone not acquainted with journalists could be forgiven for assuming that they must talk something like this: "I last night went to bed early because I this morning had to catch an early flight." That, at any rate, is how many of them write.'

In a quality newspaper, no one actually ever does anything: they are always 'set to' do it. Politicians do not say, but 'insist'. A series of proposals is a 'raft of measures' that may 'signal' a 'crackdown' or its close relative, a 'clampdown'. If even slightly noteworthy, such measures are 'key', 'major' or 'landmark'; more significant ones may be 'flagship'. But if the writer disapproves of them, they are 'controversial'. Prices do not rise but are 'hiked', which may 'fuel' a 'spiral'.

The trouble is that, as Bruce Campbell found in *The Evil Dead*, as soon as you kill one monster another horror emerges

---

@mpk 'sim card' rather than 'SIM card'? Seriously?

to take its place. As it charged across the jungle of our pages, the phrase 'elephant in the room' was used to describe, in the *Guardian* alone, climate change, anti-Americanism, Iraq, Jimmy Greaves, race, religion, Catholicism, Islam, Andrew Neil, fatness, thinness, trade figures, policy, lack of policy, Hitler, Stalinism, and Tony Blair's departure from office. We had just about got elephants in the room under control when variations on 'eye-watering' began to make their appearance. Oddly, the adjective seems to be applied only to money ('eye-watering sums'), whereas the adverb is more versatile ('an eye-wateringly beautiful woman', 'an eye-wateringly sharp sauvignon').

More recently, the perfectly innocent old word 'before' has become an endangered species because no journalist can resist replacing it with the dreaded 'ahead of'. It started with sports writers but no one is safe. I have nothing against mixing 'ahead of' with 'before' for variety, but routinely using the former when the latter is clearly called for can sound odd, if not perverse: 'Why else would they hurriedly concoct their own "Confucius peace prize", a day *ahead of* the ceremony in Oslo?' appeared in a leading article; 'university candidates are racing to submit their applications *ahead of* the tripling of tuition fees' in a news story. It sounds particularly inappropriate when the event being referred is imminent: 'I found myself surrounded by the likes of Greg Dyke, Rob Brydon and Badly Drawn Boy at a BFI reception for Springsteen *ahead of* a screening of his new documentary.'

Buzzwords – 'trope' is another recent one – are like the latest smartphone: once one writer or broadcaster has used it, they all want one. The second decade of the 21st

---

@guardianstyle Yes. Like laser, radar etc, or do you capitalise them as well?

century has been notable for the rise of the 'national treasure'. Originally a figure who enjoyed the affection of a large part of the nation – Clare Balding, Stephen Fry and Joanna Lumley, say – the term has now been extended to anyone about whom the writer can't think of anything more original to say. Recent national treasures include the cricketer Jonathan Trott, broadcaster Eddie Mair, actor Miriam Margolyes, writer Stephen Poliakoff, the late astronomer Sir Patrick Moore, and Rupert Murdoch's late mother, Dame Elisabeth. You do not have to be a person to attain national treasure status: the band Madness, the Channel 4 programme *Time Team*, the BBC, the Commonwealth War Graves Commission, the Irish Hurling League final and the Jamaican boys' and girls' athletics championships have all done so. For once, the papers are unanimous: they all love national treasures – 1,070 of them, in total, appeared in the 12 months to June 2013.

Well, people have to write something and it's not always possible to come up with inspiring original phrases. But the problem with cliches is that the readers can tell your heart isn't really in it if all you can do is churn out the same old phrases. Take Marmite. Or leave it. According to the newspapers, repaying a 2006 Marmite marketing campaign many times over, there is no middle way: it is compulsory to love or hate not just Marmite but also, among other phenomena, Boris Johnson and Ken Livingstone (fair enough), Twitter (perhaps), Lily Allen and Shirley Bassey (really? I quite like them both but I'm not that bothered either way). Which, come to think of it, is how I feel about Marmite.

@chrishughes01 Amazing, @guardianstyle is on Twitter. Must ask for their take on wowzers/wowsers

How Many Double-Decker Buses in Wales?

Let's have some new cliches.
SAMUEL GOLDWYN

Did you know that the bacon eaten in the UK every year is the equivalent in weight of 50 blue whales? That's a lot of bacon. Although oddly, 50 whales doesn't sound all that many. So it's an unhelpful comparison. When 'ecoists' (Jeremy Clarkson's word) described a slab of ice that had broken away from Antarctica as 'the size of Luxembourg', Jezza took issue with them in his *Sun* column, pointing out that the standard units of measurement in the UK are double-decker London buses, football pitches and Wales. He could have added the Isle of Wight, Olympic-sized swimming pools and Wembley stadiums to the list.

Such comparisons crop up all the time. So often, in fact, that I devised a system of abbreviations:

- SoW (size of Wales);
- SoB (size of Belgium);
- OSPs (Olympic swimming pools); and
- DDBs (double-decker buses).

So instead of telling us that Botswana is 'twice the size of Wales' (*Daily Telegraph*), it might simply have said Botswana = 2 SoWs. Thus, the Kruger National Park in South Africa measures 1 SoW (*Daily Telegraph* again), as do Lesotho (*London Evening Standard*) and Israel (*The Times*), whereas Lake Nzerakera in Tanzania is 2 SoBs (the *Observer*). When the *Guardian*'s G2 revealed that all the gold ever mined would make a cube the size of 'a stack of Routemaster buses four deep, four high and four long', my formula would render

---

it much more handily as 4×4×4 DDBs. When we reported 'Isle of Wight-sized asteroid killed dinosaurs, scientists say', a reader calculated: 'So 1bn Hiroshimas = 1 (Isle of Wight) × 20 (speeding bullets). Who needs $E=mc^2$?'

Sometimes, however, the most carefully calibrated calculations can go awry. We learn from the *Daily Telegraph* that Helmand province in Afghanistan is 'four times the size of Wales', only to find in the same publication a few weeks later that it has apparently shrunk to 'the size of Wales'.

If you think this is all an Olympic swimming pool-sized storm in a teacup, along with calculations of how far into space the hotdogs served at a Cup final would stretch, I agree that they are relatively harmless. But also meaningless, even for people like me who have actually been to Wales (though not, alas, on a double-decker bus) and Belgium – which measures, by the way, 1.5 SoWs.

Lazy, cliched and impossible to visualise. No, not the journalists who dream up this nonsense – well, not necessarily – but the comparisons. We need alternatives. I suggest quite big, big, and very big.

Cliche abuse

Irritation factor: 7/10
Frequency of error: 10/10
Misused by: all journalists

Typical example:

> *If 'heart of darkness' appears anywhere in a story, you can be sure of one thing: it's about Africa.*

@JulietDJ Is 'playwrighting' kosher? Spelling/use as a verb feels wrong!

It's the Subs Wot Write Them: Headlines

Textron Inc. Makes Offer To Screw Co. Stockholders
HEADLINE IN AMERICAN NEWSPAPER

I've been a bit grumpy in the last couple of chapters so to cheer us all up I'm going to look at headlines, the best of which everyone can enjoy, whatever paper they read. In a moment, the best headline of all time. And it isn't 'The Queen in London: Phones her Mother' (*Daily Telegraph*) or 'World War II's greatest secret – ADOLF HITLER WAS A WOMAN' (*Sunday Sport*). Some of the most fondly remembered headlines are apocryphal: it is a myth that *Guardian* reports about the explorer Vivian Fuchs ever carried the headline 'Fuchs Off To Antarctic'. The following did, however, appear: 'Sir Vivian Fuchs For Antarctic' (6 December 1963) and 'Sir Vivian Fuchs At Palace' (16 May 1968).

Headline writing is much harder than it seems. As with a completed crossword, you may look at the result and think it's obvious, but I can assure you it's not at all like that when you have a big black hole in a page just five minutes before the deadline and have to write one when the editor is looking impatiently over your shoulder. Subeditors (subs) have many tasks in their role at the heart of the news operation, particularly in the new digital age of web journalism, but the best are distinguished, as they always have been, by the ability to write a sharp headline in a hurry.

The term 'crash blossoms' has been used to describe headlines that are ambiguous, typically because they contain words that could be either a verb or a noun. The term comes from a headline in *Japan Today*: 'Violinist Linked to JAL Crash Blossoms' (her father had died in the crash, but her career was blossoming). Looked at from another perspective, a headline such as 'Landmine claims dog UK arms firm' shows how remarkably flexible English can be – a language that defies our expectations by providing a grammatical sentence despite apparently containing, in defiance of everything we were taught in school, six nouns and no verb.

The most notorious headline of all may well be 'GOTCHA' (the *Sun*, first edition only, 4 May 1982), celebrating the sinking of the Argentinian battleship ARA *General Belgrano* in the Falklands War. First recorded in written usage as 'Gotcher!' (in 1932), and defined by the OED as 'a representation of the colloquial or vulgar pronunciation of (I have) got you', its use by the *Sun* followed an exclamation by a senior editor 'Gotcha, Argies!' when news came through of the sinking. The editor, pronouncing him a genius, adopted it as the splash headline, according to *Stick It Up Your Punter! The Rise and Fall of the 'Sun'* by Peter Chippindale and Chris Horrie.

That it was changed after a single edition shows that even for the *Sun* in its 80s heyday, there was such a thing as going too far.

Less controversially, 'IT'S THE *SUN* WOT WON IT' is an interesting example of an it-cleft construction, so called because it 'cleaves' a sentence into two clauses, the main clause 'it's the *Sun*' and the relative clause 'wot won it'. The aim is to highlight the former. Compare it with 'The *Sun* won it', which is about as flat as the support won by John Major

---

@scandb Shouldn't that be Internet?

at the event being depicted, the 1997 general election. The word 'wot' began life in written form in the second world war catchphrase 'wot no … ?' protesting about shortages. The headline has been much parodied, including in this one (written by me) on the front page of the *Guardian* 15 years later: 'It's the *Sun* wot's switched sides to Labour.' Perhaps the OED had my effort in mind when it expanded its definition of 'wot' to: 'now also in extended humorous use'.

My favourite headlines usually involve a play on words, typically from well-known quotations or expressions, lightly tweaked, such as 'Book lack in Ongar' (funding cuts hit Essex libraries), 'Bad light stops plays' (an open-air theatre performance is called off because it goes dark early), 'Flo quiets the Dons' (a footballer named Jostein Flo scores two goals against Wimbledon), 'Where there's muck there's bras' (a farmer's wife launches her own lingerie business from a barn), and 'Drop dead, gorgeous' (office jealousy). Of the thousands I must have written, the one that gave me most pleasure was on a tiny 100-word story revealing that the young John Lennon had been a nature lover: 'I fed the newts today, oh boy.' (A possible alternative would have been 'Give peas a chance'.) And if they make you groan, I quote Jonathan Swift in my defence: 'Punning is a talent which no man affects to despise, but he that is without it.'

The best headline of all time? It's a tie between the *Sun* and the *Liverpool Echo*. Inverness Caledonian Thistle (nickname: Caley), a Highland football club only formed in 1994, faced the mighty Celtic at their Parkhead ground six years later in the Scottish FA Cup, and to everyone's amazement beat the former European Cup winners 3–1. The *Sun*'s headline: 'SUPER CALEY GO BALLISTIC, CELTIC ARE ATROCIOUS'. Why a tie? In the 1970s, the *Echo* described a brilliant performance by the Liverpool player Ian Callaghan against Queens Park Rangers with this headline: 'SUPER CALLY GOES BALLISTIC, QPR ATROCIOUS'. After everything I've said about cliches, I am loth to use one … but perhaps, when it comes to head-line writing, great minds think alike.

CHAPTER II

All Your Base Are Belong to Us

Social or antisocial media? How the internet has transformed language

> *The web, then, or the pattern, a web at once sensuous and logical, an elegant and pregnant texture: that is style, that is the foundation of the art of literature.*
> ROBERT LOUIS STEVENSON

> *All your base are belong to us ... You have no chance to survive make your time.*
> INTERNET MEME QUOTING THE JAPANESE VIDEO GAME ZERO WING

When I joined a new newspaper called the *Independent* a few months before its launch in 1986, we were very proud of our state-of-the-art computer system – we had all been using type-writers and editing with pen and paper until not long before. The mainframe Atex computer filled the large basement and if everyone pressed the 'HNJ' key (which hyphenated and justi-fied the text of a story) at the same time, the office shook and the system slowed almost to a halt. We loved it. And what we loved most was the electronic mailing system, which enabled us to send messages on our shiny new screens.

No one gave a thought to security as we slagged off our bosses and flirted shamelessly with each other. Around half the male staff had decided to fall in love with the same woman, so spent most of their time composing verse in an attempt to impress her. What no one realised was how pathetically easy it was to hack into the system (not a concept we had even heard of) and in no time all the messages, including the poetry, were on display in an open file for anyone to read. This had a cooling effect on office ardour.

All that seems centuries, rather than decades, ago in this age where we take it for granted that we can communicate instantly with anyone, anywhere in the world, whenever we like, via email, text message, Skype, Twitter, Facebook and numerous other social media sites. (Or give them a quick call.) The internet changes so quickly that by the time you read this some new phenomenon may have made the currently most popular sites look about as cutting edge as that old Atex system.

Pity the poor linguist trying to produce an up-to-date book about the subject. David Crystal wrote *Language and the Internet* in 2001, and by the time he came to revise it in 2006 a third of the web addresses he had included no longer existed. It was only a dozen years ago but already that first edition resembles a historical document. And even the second one predates Twitter and the explosion of social media. What did not change in those years was the author's conviction that the language of the internet – 'Netspeak' – is a variety of English that can be analysed just as linguists analyse speech and writing, regional and class dialects, scientific, legal and other 'occupational genres', and creative expression. Netspeak shares qualities with both writing and speaking, but Crystal sees it as a 'third medium', with distinctive features in spelling

---

@guardianstyle Pensioner: a reader notes that this term is never used to describe, say, Michael Caine or Rupert Murdoch, just the 'little people' ...

and punctuation and an enormous vocabulary of its own. Just think of the new words and new meanings for existing words – from ebook and email to mouse and spam; from blog and tweet to cyberspace and world wide web.

Some people, including those who use the net and social media all the time, lament how they are lowering standards of English. Robert McCrum of the *Observer* referred in 2013 to 'the violence the internet does to the English language' and 'abuse and impoverishment of English online (notably, in blogs and emails)'. I don't know who emails Robert but the ones I get are much like the letters I have always received: some are well written, some are poorly written, and most are in between. And there are lots of beautifully fashioned blogs. The problem may be that as there is just so much more material on the web, there is bound to be more that's bad – as well as more that's good.

Edward R Murrow, the American broadcaster memorably portrayed by David Strathairn in George Clooney's film *Good Night, and Good Luck*, said of television in 1958: 'This instrument can teach, it can illuminate; yes, and it can even inspire. But it can do so only to the extent that humans are determined to use it to those ends ... There is a great ... battle to be fought against ignorance, intolerance and indifference. This weapon of television could be useful.' (He might have thought differently if he had seen *Take Me Out*.) The US journalist Paul Brandus has suggested that much the same could be said of new media, which can be a force for good or ill. It all depends on how you use them.

Yes, there are trolls lurking under the bridge, waiting to jump out and provoke, harass, offend and even abuse. Some

---

@guardianstyle ... so it is better to describe someone as a retired banker, powerboat racer, homemaker etc than a 'pensioner' and never 'old age pensioner'.

writers have learned that it takes a thick skin, and a strong stomach, to read the comments under their blogposts. But this is the price we pay for media that encourage engagement and dialogue where once they dispensed wisdom from on high and readers could take it or leave it. I think the price is worth paying.

My KZ, Ur BF

> *And I wanna know what happened to your boyfriend,*
> *'cause he was looking at me like 'Whoa!'*
> *Yeah right before the kitchen was a dust bowl, and*
> *tossing me the keys …*
> EVERYTHING EVERYTHING, 'MY KZ, UR BF'

I love everything, everything, about this song, not least because it illustrates how text messaging – once dismissed as 'penmanship for illiterates' in, sad to say, the *Guardian* – can be elevated to an art form. If you have ever been to a party, and if you know that 'KZ' and 'BF' are abbreviations of keys and boyfriend, then you already have a story from the song title – in just a few characters and spaces – that you can take wherever your imagination chooses to go. But 'KZ' is also short for 'kill zone', and Everything Everything embark on a journey into destruction and chaos, perhaps caused by a terrorist attack, a world of 'everything just coming through the windows' where 'people say the army's on fire'. This complex, disturbing tour de force ends with the compelling line: 'It's like we're sitting with our parachutes on, but the airport's gone.'

@automathic Is it ok to use 'opined' for reported speech in meeting notes?

A few years ago, John Humphrys was warning in the *Daily Mail*, rather less eloquently:

> *Mary had a mobile, she texted day and night.*
> *But when it came to her exams she'd forgotten how*
> *to write.*

From this widely held point of view, texters were 'vandals who are doing to our language what Genghis Khan did to his neighbours 800 years ago. They are destroying it.' The arrival of SMS (short message service) provoked at times an extreme reaction and dire warnings that young people would no longer be able to communicate normally, but only in textspeak. And then only if they managed to avoid serious thumb injury. Older people often go on like this, perhaps through jealousy. Ogden Nash wrote 60 years ago:

> *The pidgin talk the youthful use*
> *Bypasses conversation.*
> *I can't believe the code they choose*
> *Is a means of communication.*

If they are bothered about any of this, which I doubt, young people can take comfort from the fact that similar fears have been expressed throughout history. Like other children of the 1950s and 60s, I lived with the constant concerns of grownups that my favourite TV programmes and pop songs would corrupt my morals, rot my brain and leave me speaking in American slang. Doubtless 40,000 years ago the Palaeolithic edition of the *Mail* would have warned how cave paintings were

@guardianstyle Only if you want to sound pompous and silly.

corrupting the young and saying 'call *that* art?'. And doubtless one day today's young people will be moaning about how standards have fallen since the golden age of the early 21st century when they texted each other in perfect English all the time.

In *Txtng: The Gr8 Db8*, David Crystal (yes, him again, but no other linguist seems prepared to take on such a range of contemporary subjects) demonstrates that all the offences against English of which texters are routinely accused have been commonplace and acceptable in the language for centuries. English is rich in useful initialisms: AKA, DVD, NB, RIP and many more. Most people are familiar with the tantalising Valentine's Day card message SWALK ('sealed with a loving kiss') – or, in the case of Alan Bennett in the 1960s comedy *Beyond the Fringe*, BURMA ('be upstairs ready my angel'), which turned out to be inappropriate because the object of his affections, a Miss Prosser, lived in a flat.

Omission of letters is common, too: in texting, '2nite', perhaps; in more formal use, Mr and Mrs. Rebuses (Latin for 'by things') like B4 and CUL8R have also been around for hundreds of years, and non-standard spellings such as 'wot' (1829) and 'luv' (1898) date from the 19th century. Finally, shortened words commonly found in text messages – uni, for example – are no different from bus, exam, vet and numerous similar examples. Jonathan Swift, the John Humphrys of his day, found such practices 'barbarous'.

In fact, only a small proportion of text language conforms to the stereotype. For example, just a handful of initialisms – such as IMHO, 'in my humble opinion', and LOL, 'laughing out loud' (or, if you are David Cameron texting the editor of the *Sun* during a general election campaign,

---

@Morus1516 When 'way to say it' determines 'way it's written'?

'lots of love') – have caught on. One survey showed that as little as 6 per cent of text messages comprised abbreviations. As with email, older users have adopted texting, and traditional orthography (with a few shortcuts) is widespread.

Every minute, the world's mobile phone users send more than 15 million text messages. There is no evidence that any of them have forgotten how to write.

140 Characters in Search of a Tweet

> *The trouble with Twitter, the instantness of it –*
> *too many tweets might make a twat.*
>
> DAVID CAMERON

I know what you're thinking: 'he's not wrong there' ... When it comes to technology, the prime minister is about as 'chillaxed' as a nun at a hen night. LOL. But when I first heard about Twitter, I also had doubts. It sounded silly. If you want to know what everyone is doing, all the time – which I don't – that's what status updates on Facebook are for. But Twitter, I now realise, is the best thing since 7 July 1928, when the Chillicothe Baking Company of Chillicothe, Missouri, produced the first loaf of 'Kleen Maid Sliced Bread'.

About 750,000 people follow @guardiannews on Twitter. There is no better way to get quick, up-to-the-minute news than a Twitter feed; further information or analysis is available at the click of a link. And there is much more to the microblogging site than just news. There's following Justin Bieber's every move, along with 40 million others. But if that doesn't

@**guardianstyle** Yes: an LSE student;
a London School of Economics student.

appeal, Twitter provides wonderful opportunities to learn things from people you would never otherwise have come into contact with. You can have your say about anything, from *Britain's Got Talent* to the budget, in real time, without the mediation of editors or (normally) censors. You can share recipes with strangers or exchange photographs of butterflies with fellow enthusiasts anywhere in the world. You can make friends and, perhaps, influence people. There may be a downside. Paul Brandus (175,000 followers) says: 'I'm bombarded daily with angry, insulting, condescending tweets from people questioning my manhood, patriotism, and intelligence.' He thinks it's worth it. I must be lucky because the 40,000-plus people who follow the feed I edit, @guardianstyle, are unfailingly polite and waste precious characters thanking me for my grammatical advice, even when it's sarky or snarky.

@GrammarGirl (Mignon Fogarty) has produced a useful online guide for those new to Twitter:

• Don't start posts with 'I am'.
• Use capitalisation (lowercase doesn't save characters) and basic punctuation.
• Don't use abbreviations that make you sound like a 12-year-old.
• Use contractions and shortened word forms such as nite and thru.
• Use numerals and symbols such as & and @.
• Provide shortened links and context.
• And, finally, 'if you can't say it in 140 characters, re-evaluate whether you should be posting it at Twitter'.

@guardianstyle A reader emails to say we should have written 'Brown is hoist WITH [not BY] his own petard' (Martin Kettle column) ...

One piece of advice she might have added, which applies to anything you do on the internet: DON'T SHOUT.

Twitter forces you to write concisely, and it's amazing what has been achieved in 140 characters or fewer. Here is a fine Twitter poem, 'Low Pay Piecework', posted by the American poet and critic Robert Pinsky:

> *The 5th-grade teacher & her followers –*
> *5 classes, 28 in each, all hers:*
> *140_different_characters.*
> @ROBERTPINSKY

Such economy: he still had 42 characters to spare.

Haikus are perfectly suited to Twitter. The highlight of National Grammar Day 2013 (in the US; we don't have one in the UK, although I am thinking of starting one) was a haiku competition. My three favourites, all of which should resonate with readers of this book, were:

> *Dear yoga teacher:*
> *If you say 'lay down' once more,*
> *I'll hurt you. No lie.*
> @FRITINANCY (NANCY FRIEDMAN)

> *Litter your lines with*
> *'literally'; I'll go nuts.*
> *(Figuratively.)*
> @ACTUALLYHOLLY (HOLLY ASHWORTH)

@guardianstyle ... Rather more interesting, we learn, is that petard (a small bomb) comes from the Middle French for 'to break wind'

> *Grammar does its thing*
> *In spite of sticklers' wishes.*
> *Omit needless rules.*
> @STANCAREY

If you are not familiar with Twitter, I hope the tweets reproduced in this book will give you a sense of its appeal: @guardianstyle has brought me as much pleasure, and taught me as much, as anything else I have done in journalism.

CHAPTER 12

Let Your Yeah Be Yeah

Keep it simple: some rules of good writing

> *But let your communication be, Yea, yea; Nay, nay: for*
> *whatsoever is more than these cometh of evil.*
> MATTHEW 5:37 (AUTHORISED VERSION)

> *Let your yeah be yeah and your no be no, now.*
> JIMMY CLIFF, 'LET YOUR YEAH BE YEAH AND YOUR NO BE NO'

Like *Sgt. Pepper's Lonely Hearts Club Band*, we are getting
very near the end. It's time to sum up.

Percy Bysshe Shelley packed a lot into his 29 years. As
well as poetry, he invented many useful words and phrases,
including 'national anthem'. He also offered this sound
advice to writers: 'In order to move men to true sympathy
we must use the familiar language of men.'

Whether you are writing a get-well-soon card, a Facebook
message, a 15,000-word dissertation on the reflexive pronoun
'myself', a tweet, a letter to the building society asking why
your nest egg has actually shrunk under their stewardship, or
a note to slip inside someone's satchel saying 'my friend really
likes you', you want it to be as clear as possible. Reading
to someone about crocodiles, as David Copperfield did
to Peggotty, and then discovering that they 'had a cloudy

impression that they were some sort of vegetable' would not be a good result.

As Stephen King says: 'Language does not always have to wear a tie and lace-up shoes.' If you are not careful, formal writing can descend into jargon and you will end up sounding like, say, the millionaire chief executive of an international bank. In teaching subeditors to write better headlines I encourage them to write the way they would speak. No one in a pub says things like 'Did you see that last night Clegg slammed Cameron in a dramatic power bid?'

CP Scott, editor of the *Manchester Guardian* for six decades and best known for the maxim 'comment is free but facts are sacred', wanted the paper to appeal to the average man and woman through the use of plain, unostentatious language. He was a fierce subeditor who would change woolly phrases like 'seaward journey to the great metropolis' to 'voyage to London'. Like Scott, you need to keep asking 'what does this actually mean?', whether reading someone else's words or your own.

One of the most common barriers to clear communication is ambiguity. Sometimes it is hard to avoid in English. In the question 'have you seen our new French teacher?' there is no way to differentiate between a French person who teaches, say, music, and a teacher of any nationality who teaches French. You would have to recast the sentence. In spoken English, there would be no ambiguity because of the stress on *French* if the teacher taught French and the first syllable of *tea*cher if the teacher were French.

Be on the lookout for words that could mean more than one thing. If you can think of an even mildly amusing double meaning, use a different word. For example, 'Miliband appealed to his backbenchers' might mean that he made a plea to them, or, conceivably, that they liked him. There's always a way round such problems, in this case 'Miliband made an appeal to his backbenchers' or similar. Does 'it is the most beautiful castle in France, if not the whole of Europe' mean 'and maybe in the whole of Europe' or 'but not in the whole of Europe'? I have no idea. Rephrase it.

Sometimes you have to rely entirely on the context: 'a curious man' could be naturally inquisitive, or have two heads, and even in spoken English there is no way to distinguish between the two. If my dog, however, can work out the difference between 'lead on, Lupin!' (lead the way) and 'lead on, Lupin!' (come and have your lead on) you should be able to manage.

Rules of Good Writing

Let us, when we sit down to write, take a solemn oath to say exactly what we mean and to say nothing more, to use the simplest words that will serve our purpose, and to use as few of them as we can.

CEM JOAD

George Orwell, who thought 'a mixture of vagueness and sheer incompetence is the most marked characteristic of modern English prose' – so the 1940s was no 'golden age', then – proposed six rules of good writing that books like this always quote. Most people will know these off by heart by now, so with due respect to Orwell I will add a few of my own, and some from the late American writer William Safire (of 'Whoppers Junior' fame).

Orwell

- 'Never use a metaphor, simile or other figure of speech which you are used to seeing in print.' (So much for the elephant in the room.)
- 'Never use a long word where a short one will do.' (Or as Mark Twain put it: 'I never write metropolis for seven cents because I can get the same money for city.')
- 'If it is possible to cut a word out, always cut it out.' (If Orwell had had a good subeditor, this one would have read: 'If you can cut a word out, cut.')
- 'Never use the passive where you can use the active.' (Although he does so very effectively in *Animal Farm*.)
- 'Never use a foreign phrase, a scientific word or a jargon word if you can think of an everyday English equivalent.'
- 'Break any of these rules sooner than say anything outright barbarous.'

Marsh

- **Use plain language.** Don't just take my word for it: Aristotle (384–322BC) said: 'Clearness is secured by using the words that are current and ordinary.' Words and phrases that people use to make themselves sound important succeed only in making them sound self-important. No one will be impressed if you say 'resides', 'prior to', 'commence' or 'purchase' when you mean lives, before, start or buy. 'There is nothing in philosophy which

---

@Skepticscalpel Re: alcohol. Hangover, hang over or hang-over? Hungover, hung over or hung-over?

could not be said in everyday language,' as Henri Bergson ejaculated. Sorry, 'said'.

- **Be concise.** A point emphasised by writers through the ages. In Charles Kingsley's *The Water-Babies*, there is a proposal to tax long words. Blaise Pascal apologised for a letter being long, explaining: 'I have not had the time to make it shorter.' 'Brevity is the soul of wit', according to Shakespeare (and 'the sister of talent', Chekhov added). What's the best Hollywood pitch of all time? Four words: 'SNAKES ON A PLANE.'

- **Avoid euphemism.** You can still be polite – 'where's the bathroom, please?' will be preferable to 'where's the bog?' in most social situations – but trying to put a gloss on an uncomfortable truth can cause misunderstanding and often more offence than speaking plainly. Horses, like people, die. When the *Guardian* reported of Raisa (the horse lent by police to the then chief executive of News International) that 'the Met said the horse had subsequently passed away,' it is not clear whose feelings we were trying to spare. When a politician or civil servant say they are being 'economical with the *actualité*', it all sounds very charming but what they mean is they are lying (and not very good at French, as *actualité* does not mean 'truth'). And as we have seen, the military use euphemism to conceal the horrors of war.

- **Don't try too hard.** The *New York Times* editor Theodore M Bernstein coined 'monologophobe' to describe 'a writer who would rather walk naked in front of Saks Fifth Avenue than be caught using the same word more than once in three lines'. Writers in search of something called elegant variation will refer to Dalí as 'the moustachioed surrealist', Ireland 'the cockatoo-shaped landmass' or ice-cream 'the iced dessert' rather than repeat Dalí, Ireland or ice-cream. At the *Guardian*, we call these Povs, as in 'popular orange vegetable', an 'elegant variation' on carrot. About as elegant as John Sergeant and Ann Widdecombe performing the duet from the second act of *Giselle*.

- **Think of the reader.** For instance, the word 'that' can often be left out, but there are times when it is useful: you tend to read a sentence such as 'he said nothing by way of an explanation would be forthcoming' as 'he said nothing by way of an explanation', so then you have to go back to reread it, which is extremely annoying. Avoid this by inserting one little word: 'he said *that* nothing by way of an explanation would be forthcoming.'

- **Read it aloud.** It is amazing what a difference this can make; for example, it will tell you when you need to use 'that'. You will get a better feel for the rhythm of the sentence, tautologies – such as 'new innovation' – will leap off the page, and words not earning their keep will reveal themselves. Samuel Johnson advised: 'Read over your compositions, and where ever you meet with a passage which you think is particularly fine, strike it out.' This seems a bit extreme. But reading aloud can help you spot the bits that people skip, as Elmore Leonard put it.

- **Check for mistakes.** Are there any rogue apostrophe's? If a word can be spelt more than one way, don't be *phased* by it: do a quick check. Some very common errors are: its or it's; chose or choose; lay or laid; lead or led; lets or let's;

@scandb Is it Lego or LEGO? Should you ever call individual bricks Legos?

their, there or they're; whose or who's. (And for Tesco executives: men's or mens, women's or womens, kids' or kids.)
- **And one more …** When you come across the phrase 'best
  avoided by careful writers', a prissy expression found in
  many grammar manuals, do whatever it is they are saying
  you should avoid. There will probably be nothing wrong
  with it.

Safire

- 'Do not put statements in the negative form.'
- 'Proofread carefully to see if you words out.'
- 'If you reread your work, you can find on rereading a
  great deal of repetition can be avoided by rereading and
  editing.'
- 'And don't start a sentence with a conjunction.'
- 'Writing carefully, dangling participles must be avoided.'
- 'Take the bull by the hand and avoid mixing metaphors.'
- 'Everyone should be careful to use a singular pronoun
  with singular nouns in their writing.'
- 'Last but not least, avoid cliches like the plague.'

The Quest Continues

> *It seemed as if we were within reach of consistency, that
> grammarian's dream of perfection.*
> KINGSLEY AMIS

Is grammatical perfection possible? Of course not. If even
Dr Johnson conceded that he could not secure the language

from 'corruption and decay' or clear the world of 'folly, vanity, and affectation', what chance have I got? But in any case, it's impossible to say what perfection, or even consistency, would look like. Despite the efforts of some of Johnson's contemporaries and their successors, some of whom are still gerund-grinding away today, you can't freeze a language – it will continue to evolve, whether you embrace or resist the changes. As native speakers we all follow a set of rules that enable us to communicate with and understand each other. But there are lots of Englishes, and even within Standard English there are many choices where no hard-and-fast rule can be set down. And even if everyone did use the same 'perfect' English, how dull life would be.

This doesn't mean I feel it's all been a waste, a tragic failure to live up to those heady days in Mrs Birtles' class when I believed that, with a little help from *The New First Aid in English*, I could change the world. James Thurber wrote: 'With sixty staring me in the face, I have developed inflammation of the sentence structure and definite hardening of the paragraphs.' I know exactly how he felt. But I recently met someone at a party who casually mentioned – *without knowing what my job was* – that there seemed to be fewer spelling mistakes in 'the Grauniad' these days. It's a start.

BIBLIOGRAPHY

My Top 20

Here is an eclectic selection of books and websites about language that aren't boring. I got the idea from Kingsley Amis, who in his own *The King's English* said: 'What I give here is less a bibliography in the recommended-reading sense than a talkative list of those other books that I found indispensable or at least useful in writing this one.' Some of the authors, including Amis, would probably be horrified to find themselves rubbing shoulders in this list with writers who stand for everything they oppose. But it's not healthy to read only stuff you agree with.

Please read to the end – it's like one of those films where there is a little surprise after the credits. Although not as funny as *Airplane!*. And don't call me Shirley.

20

The New First Aid in English, Angus Maciver
(Hodder, 2nd edition, 2004)
My first love. In grammar, anyway. *First Aid in English*, written by Angus Maciver, a Scottish teacher, was published in 1938. Its successor remains a wonderful introduction to the English language for children and non-native speakers, packed with information that is hard to find elsewhere and

exercises that I defy you not to enjoy. If you took the 11-plus, this is your chance to relive it.

What it says: 'My clock has gone wrong and chimes three times at one o'clock, four times at two o'clock, and so on. It is also half-an-hour fast. What is the correct time when the clock has just chimed eight?'

19

How to Write Better English, Robert Allen
(Penguin, 2005)
A thorough guide to the basics, written by the editor-in-chief of the Penguin English Dictionary. Lots of useful examples, but don't expect too many laughs.

What he says: 'When you look out of the window at the pouring rain and exclaim "What a lovely day!", you are using a form of irony.'

18

Eats, Shoots & Leaves, Lynne Truss
(Profile Books, 2003)
... and leaves many of her arguments full of holes, it's tempting to add. Like an undercooked curate's egg, sloppy in parts. But like just about every writer and journalist I know, I wish I had had the idea for this book.

What she says: 'The big final rule for the comma is one that you won't find in any books by grammarians. It is quite easy

---

@SamanthaMarcy Web site, web site, Website, or website?

to remember, however. The rule is: don't use commas like a stupid person.'
See also (not by the same author): Eats, Shites & Leaves: Crap English and How to Use It (Michael O'Mara Books Ltd, 2004).

17

Strictly English, Simon Heffer
(Random House, 2010)
A valiant, if doomed, attempt to turn the clock back 100 years which taught me that you can like and respect someone even if you disagree with him about nearly everything.
What he warns: '*Warn* has not developed into an intransitive verb, despite an enormous effort by semi-literates over the centuries to make it so. One can *warn* somebody, and one can *warn against* something, but one cannot simply *warn*. If for some reason one cannot use an object, use the phrase *give warning*.'
See also: The Telegraph Style Guide.

16

Language Myths, edited by Laurie Bauer and Peter Trudgill
(Penguin, 1998)
A bracing antidote to prescriptiveness, with 21 essays debunking what the authors regard as myths – such as that

words should not be allowed to change their meaning, women talk more than men, and people in the Appalachians speak like Shakespeare. I somehow doubt, though, that Professor Trudgill would have used *imply* and *infer* interchangeably, as he recommends to others, when he applied for the various chairs he has held.

What they say: 'We believe that, on the whole, linguists have not been good at informing the general public about language ... Why is it that if you look at something written by the most influential linguists ... you will not necessarily come away any wiser?'

15

The Etymologicon, Mark Forsyth
(Icon Books, 2011)
Among the many intriguing, if useless, things I learned from this fascinating book are that *avocado* is derived from the Aztec for testicle, *bizarre* from the Basque for beard, and *dormouse*, charmingly, from the French *dormeuse* ('she who sleeps').

What he says: 'The ancient Indians called their dads *pitar*, and the Greeks called their dads *pater*, and the Romans called them *pater*. The Germans, though, started pronouncing the letter P in a very funny way that made it sound more like an F. So they called their male parent *fater*, and we call him *father*, because English is descended from Old German.'

See also: The Horologicon: A Day's Jaunt Through the Lost Words of the English Language.

***

@KickyVell The best thing on Twitter today BY FAR is @ guardianstyle #ff #wordgeekery

14

Language Log

http://itre.cis.upenn.edu/~myl/languagelog/

The prolific Mark Liberman and Geoffrey K Pullum curate a website that combines intimidating knowledge with humour and a no-nonsense writing style. Some of the comments from their readers can sound a little smug.

What they say: 'Whenever you hear someone starting to say something that begins with "The X have no word for Y," or "The X have N different words for Y," never listen to them, and always check your wallet to make sure it's still there.'

See also: Far from the Madding Gerund and Other Dispatches from Language Log; Hand-Clappin' Foot Stompin' Funky-Butt Live! (LP) by Geno Washington & the Ram Jam Band.

13

Mother Tongue, Bill Bryson

(Hamish Hamilton, 1990)

As you'd expect of a former subeditor (we worked alongside each other in the early days of the *Independent*), not a word is wasted in this entertaining history of how English became a global language. Full of interesting anecdotes and fascinating facts.

What he says: 'If a standard western typewriter keyboard were expanded to take in every Chinese ideograph it would have to be about 15 feet long and five feet wide.'

See also: Troublesome Words.

12

Sentence First: An Irishman's Blog about the English Language
http://stancarey.wordpress.com/
Short, quirky blogposts on often arcane language-related subjects, packed with the most surprising stories (such as how Mick Jagger entertained the director Werner Herzog with 'clever little lectures' about dialects and 'the development of the language since the late Middle Ages' on the set of *Fitzcarraldo* in Peru in 1981). I'd love to sit in front of a log fire with Stan Carey one night sharing a bottle of Irish whiskey and listening to this stuff. The blog is packed with links to other sites. Excellent tweets too. Indispensable.

What he says: 'I live in the west of Ireland, but thanks to modern technology you can read this blog (almost) anywhere. Its title is from a line spoken by the Queen in *Alice's Adventures in Wonderland*: "Sentence first – verdict afterwards." '

11

Mortal Syntax, June Casagrande
(Penguin, 2008)
As the title suggests, a funny and enjoyable read from an American journalist and writer who knows her stuff but does not take herself too seriously.

What she says: 'Once upon a time, *hopefully* meant only "in a hopeful manner" … But by the same token, *thou* used to mean "you", and *sun* used to mean "a big thing that revolves

around the Earth and will someday inflict its wrath upon us" (just as we moderns would define a Fox News satellite).'
See also: Grammar Snobs Are Great Big Meanies; It Was the Best of Sentences, It Was the Worst of Sentences.

10

Wordlady
http://katherinebarber.blogspot.co.uk/
Katherine Barber is a Canadian who blogs about words with wit and wisdom. I find I always learn something new. She often corrects my tweets, but in a tactful way.
What she says: 'Why is there a silent P in *ptarmigan*? In the late 17th century, some meddlesome person, thinking the word was derived from the Greek *ptero* (meaning feather or wing) stuck a P at the beginning to reflect its "Greek" origin. It's been there ever since.'
See also: Six Words You Never Knew Had Something to Do with Pigs.

9

Unspeak: Words are Weapons, Steven Poole
(Little, Brown, 2006)
The author, a *Guardian* colleague, writes with controlled, concentrated anger about the way those in power use language to hoodwink us. If everyone read this book, there would be rioting in the streets.

@guardianstyle Oddly, it used to be to-morrow.
A VERY LONG TIME AGO.

What he says: 'Words have consequences in the world. To adopt the phrase "ethnic cleansing" is to be complicit in mass killing.'

8

Separated by a Common Language
http://separatedbyacommonlanguage.blogspot.co.uk/
Blogging as 'Lynneguist', Lynne Murphy, reader in linguistics and English language at the University of Sussex, offers a cool, authoritative take on the differences and similarities between British and American English. When you read this blog, you realise how much time people waste getting worked up about 'Americanisms' when they could be celebrating how much fun language can be.

What she says: '*Wonk*'s entry into BrE is complicated a bit by the BrE word *wonky* (which is currently making inroads in AmE), which means "unsteady; apt to malfunction; not quite right". But that doesn't seem to be holding it back. Hail to the wonks! And to *wonk*!'

7

Invitation to Linguistics, Richard Hudson
(Blackwell, 1984)
Written for students, but a superb introduction to the subject for anyone. I was lucky enough to be taught at UCL by Dick Hudson, whose brilliant lectures were so popular that you

@suewalder Palindromes – Won ton? Not now! Do geese see God? Amy, must I jujitsu my ma? #lovelanguage

had to get there early if you wanted a seat; lots of people who were not even studying language used to come along. That charisma shines through his writing.

What he says: 'Any variety of language is a complex structure with its own rules … perfectly adapted to the needs of the community that uses it.'

See also: Sociolinguistics.

6

Waterhouse on Newspaper Style, Keith Waterhouse
(Viking, 1989)
Although it began life in the 1970s as the *Daily Mirror*'s style guide, this is no longer the 'standard guide' for journalists, as claimed on the cover; it reads more like an eloquent lament for a tabloid era that already feels as distant as the days of black-and-white television.

What he says: 'Facetiousness is not witty, for all that a well-honed pun may cause mock groans of appreciation among readers as far away from Fleet Street as Ludgate Circus.'

5

The Devil's Dictionary, Ambrose Bierce
(Neale Publishing, 1911)
Bierce, a journalist and author born in 1842, lived a colourful life: he fought in the American civil war and disappeared without trace at the age of 71 while travelling with Pancho

Villa's Mexican revolutionaries. *The Devil's Dictionary*, published in 1911, is an ironic A–Z of wit and wisdom about language, politics, religion and various other targets. Many of his aphorisms would have made wonderful tweets.

What he says: 'Scribbler, *n*. A professional writer whose views are antagonistic to one's own.'

4

The Use of English, Randolph Quirk
(Longmans, 1962)
A great British man of letters, not least for his influence on so many others (including David Crystal) at UCL, where in 1959 he established the Survey of English Usage, which continues to carry out important research in English language corpus linguistics. With three colleagues, Quirk produced the monumental *A Comprehensive Grammar of the English Language* in 1985. I prefer *The Use of English*, a warm and wise approach to descriptive grammar that set the tone for much that followed.

What he says: 'In relation to the social aspects of language, one observer has suggested that English speakers fall into three categories: the assured, the anxious, and the indifferent.'

3

The King's English, Kingsley Amis
(HarperCollins, 1997)

@adamin Do I fill in or fill out a form?

Not what you might expect if you have read his later novels. Although Amis does not suffer fools gladly, the barbs are mostly gentle and he is surprisingly liberal: for example, he criticises 'some old curmudgeon' for 'frothing on' about the use of *gay* instead of *homosexual*. By some margin the best written of any book on this list.

What he says: '*Destination* has arrived. The word retains its pompous railway-guide feel, but it is quite long and sonorous and does seem to dignify bloody awful places like Blackpool and Acapulco. Nevertheless it exemplifies a trend worth resisting.'

See also: Lucky Jim. Not a language book, but a wonderful read.

2

The Story of English in 100 Words, David Crystal
(Profile Books, 2012)
The most prolific, and in my opinion the greatest, British linguist, David Crystal could write an interesting book about people's notes for the milkman. His love and deep knowledge of language is apparent in every one of dozens of titles, nowhere more than in this book, which pulls together all his themes in a glorious history of English told in 100 words, from the earliest example of a written word in the language – *roe* – to *Twittersphere*, from *arse* to *app*, from *wicked* to *webzine*.

What he says: 'If just a fraction of the nervous energy which is currently devoted to the criticism of split infinitives and the intrusive R were devoted to the constructive promotion

@guardianstyle Either – they mean exactly the same. (See also: get on up/get on down.)

of forward-looking language activities, what might not be achieved?'

See also: Who Cares About English Usage?; *Language and the Internet*; *Txtng: The Gr8 Db8*; *The Fight for English* and numerous others, all superb.

I

The Language Instinct, Steven Pinker
(Penguin, 1994)

Inspiring, moving and profound. If you only read one book about language, apart from *For Who the Bell Tolls*, make it this one. Starting from Darwin's assertion that language is 'an instinctive tendency to acquire an art', Pinker, a cognitive scientist, develops the theme that 'people know how to talk in more or less the sense that spiders know how to spin webs'. It's an exhilarating journey.

What he says: 'To a scientist, the fundamental fact of language is its sheer improbability. Most objects in the universe – lakes, rocks, trees, worms, cows, cars – cannot talk ... I can arrange a combination of words that explains how octopuses make love or how to remove cherry stains; rearrange the words in even the most minor way, and the result is a sentence with a different meaning or, most likely of all, word salad. How are we to account for this miracle?'

See also: Words and Rules.

@guardianstyle Rotokas alphabet (Bougainville, Papua New Guinea) comprises 12 letters (A E G I K O P R S T U V) but V is sometimes written B. #lovelanguage

And finally ...

I am about to – or I am going to – die; either expression is used.

LAST WORDS OF 17TH-CENTURY FRENCH JESUIT GRAMMARIAN
DOMINIQUE BOUHOURS

@unit01 Unfollowed @FakeAPStylebook –
@guardianstyle makes me realize real grammar is
much cooler than fake grammar.

ACKNOWLEDGEMENTS

Special thanks to my wife, Anna Bawden, for literally holding the baby while I was writing this. (Yeah, I dropped the 'literally' bomb.)

Thanks to Sara Montgomery for coming up with the original idea for a 'quirky grammar book', and to my friend and colleague Amelia Hodsdon for interrupting her maternity leave to contribute to the quirky index.

Thanks also to Bas Aarts, Richard Alcock, Adi Bloom, Andy Bodle, Lindsay Davies, Jamie Fahey, Rory Foster, Elena Fysentzou, Nikki Marshall, Gary Nunn, Harriet Powney, Saptarshi Ray, Katie Roden, Maddie York, [note Oxford comma] and the nice people at Faber & Faber.

Finally, thanks to all the subeditors, past and present, who are the heart and soul of the *Guardian*. 'They also serve who do not sign their names.'

Some passages in this book have appeared in a different form on the *Guardian*'s Mind Your Language blog.

INDEX

vagueness 139–40
verb phrases 21–2, 28
verbs 21
    auxiliary 75, 130, 218
    copular 16, 22–3
    modal 130–1
    pronouns' agreement with
        72–4
    in subject–verb–object
        combination 15, 16
    transitive 16, 77
Volkovitch, Michel 95–6
Vonnegut, Kurt 95

Wain, Alex 193
Wall Street Journal 127
Walpole, Horace 105
wankers, *see* berks and wankers
Waterhouse, Keith 93
Waugh, Evelyn 103
Weather Project 201–2
Webster, Noah 110
Welsh 106
    see also languages
which vs *that* 61–2
Who Cares About English Usage?
    (Crystal) 237
who vs *whom*, subject of an object
    lesson 58–61
Widdecombe, Ann 210–11
Wierzbicka, Anna 137–8
Wilson, Thomas 191, 197
Winnie-the-Pooh, wobbly spelling
    of 109
Winterson, Jeanette 95
Wittgenstein, Ludwig 139
words:
    abbreviations 119
    American 110, 199–201
    capital letters used for 120–1
    changing meanings of 106–7
    confusion, anger or despair
        caused by, an A–Z 143–90

euphemisms 267
'Gate'-ways to meaning 124–5
    hyphenated 125–7
    idiomatic 127–8
    in IT age, *see* information
        technology
    as jargon, *see* jargon
    and journalese, *see* news: clichés
        in
    most popular 104–5
    names 117–18, 132–3
    pretentiously foreign 191–204
        passim
    pronunciation of 109, 110–11,
        135
    in Shakespeare 107
    Shaw's simplification of 110
    snowclones 123
    spelling of 109–11; *see also*
        spelling
    in technology 32, 107–8,
        207; *see also* information
        technology; jargon
    troublesome, listed 112–17
    as txt msgs 256–9
    useful stuff about, A–Z 119–41
    wonder of 103–41
    see also languages
Wurzels, posher than Bakewell
    135
Wyld, HC 35

'yeah, yeah, yeah,' overstated threat
    to existence of 'yes' from 14
Yoda, and how language strikes
    back 9, 10, 134
Yorkshiremen:
    how to annoy 121
    Nazi-confusing power of 135
Younge, Gary 42

zeugma 141
zhoosh, a showy word 190